£6.50

the BIG BOOK
of jazz piano improvisation

▶ **Tools and inspiration for creative soloing**

noah baerman

Alfred, the leader in educational publishing, and the National Keyboard Workshop, one of America's leading contemporary music schools, have joined forces to bring you the best, most progressive educational tools possible. We hope you will enjoy this book and encourage you to look for other fine products from Alfred and the National Keyboard Workshop.

GW00759907

Copyright © MMIII by Alfred Publishing Co., Inc.
All rights reserved. Printed in USA.
ISBN 0-7390-3171-6 (Book & CD)

This book was acquired, edited and produced
by Workshop Arts, Inc., the publishing arm of
the National Guitar Workshop.
Nathaniel Gunod, acquisitions and managing editor
Michael Rodman, editor
Matt Cramer, music typesetter and assistant editor
Timothy Phelps, interior design
CD recorded at Bar None Studios, Northford, CT

TABLE OF CONTENTS

ABOUT THE AUTHOR

PHOTO BY KATE TEN EYCK

Born and raised in New Haven, Connecticut, Noah Baerman began piano studies at age eight. He received his first formal jazz training at the Educational Center for the Arts in New Haven and at Jackie McLean's Artists' Collective in Hartford. There, he began his professional jazz career, including a long association with saxophonist and fellow student Jimmy Greene. Noah went on to earn bachelor's and master's degrees in jazz studies from the Mason Gross School of the Arts at Rutgers University, and also taught several jazz courses there. While at Rutgers, he spent six years under the tutelage of renowned jazz pianist Kenny Barron. Noah has worked in and around New York with a wide variety of jazz artists, and from 1994 to 1999 he co-led the jazz quartet Positive Rhythmic Force (PRF), which established itself in the jazz world through clinics, recordings and live performances. During this time, Noah was also active in the interdisciplinary arts, creating pieces employing poetry, modern dance, theater, puppetry and visual art.

Noah performs actively with his piano trio and works as a freelance jazz organist and pianist. He also directs the soul group Mr. B's Boogie Band, maintains the website www.noahjazz.com, teaches and composes. His 2003 album *Patch Kit,* a benefit album for the EDNF (Ehlers-Danlos National Foundation), features the trio of Noah, Ron Carter and Ben Riley. Noah's other books for Workshop Arts/Alfred include the three-volume *Complete Jazz Keyboard Method, Jazz Keyboard Harmony* and the *Portraits* series. Noah lives in Connecticut with his wife, visual artist Kate Ten Eyck.

DEDICATION

This book is dedicated to the memory and music of eight great jazz artists who moved on to the jam session in the sky while it was being written: J. J. Johnson (1924–2001), John Lewis (1920–2001), Joe Henderson (1937–2001), Billy Higgins (1936–2001), Tommy Flanagan (1930–2001), Shirley Scott (1934–2002), Ray Brown (1926–2002) and Lionel Hampton (1909–2002).

ACKNOWLEDGEMENTS

Thanks to Nat Gunod, Dave Smolover, Michael Rodman, Matt Cramer, Tim Phelps and everyone at NGW and Workshop Arts; to Morton Manus, Ron Manus, E. L. Lancaster, Link Harnsberger and everyone at Alfred Publishing; to Collin Tilton at Bar None Studio; to Kenny Barron, Ted Dunbar, George Raccio, Ron Carter, Ben Riley, Ralph Bowen, Jimmy Greene, Jason Berg, Sunny Jain, Ben Tedoff, Amanda Monaco, Bob Hart, Wayne Escoffery, Noah Bloom, Joanne Brackeen, Michael Mossman, Phil Schaap, Lewis Porter, William Fielder, Larry Ridley, Richard Thompson, Franya Berkman, Tyler Goodwin, George Mastrogiannis, Christine Caruso, Dawn Revett, Emily Wilson, Seth Bloom, Rachel Green, Doug Maher, Carl Knox, Caryl Johnson, Dr. Enrico Liva, Alice Schumacher, Clara Shen, Wanda Maximilien and Eva Pierrou; to the Rutgers Music Department, the Artists' Collective and ECA; to Wesleyan University's Center For the Arts, Music Department and library; to Linda, Andrew and everyone else at the EDNF; to the Ten Eyck family: Bob, Carol, Dave, Carla, Jackson, Dan, Barry, Dottie and Peter; to the Baerman family: Mom, Dad, Alison, Jennifer, Anna, Matthew, Tanja and Jonah; and to my soulful soulmate, Kate Ten Eyck.

USING THIS BOOK

The Big Book of Jazz Piano Improvisation is designed to be flexible. Should you want to work methodically through the book from beginning to end, the lessons are presented in a systematic way that enables and encourages a step-by-step learning process. If, on the other hand, you come to this book with some experience in improvisation, you can pick and choose lessons to explore new areas or reinforce those that need work. In the latter case, you're encouraged to at least take a look the surrounding sections to ensure that you've devoted proper attention to the ideas and techniques you'll need to use as building blocks.

Most of the material in this book falls into one of three categories:

1. **Toolbox (Chapters 1, 3 and 5)**
   The Toolboxes are, literally, the nuts and bolts of our study. The scales, progressions and other tools in these chapters provide the basis for the subsequent lessons. The first toolbox, which begins on page 8, includes a review of musical elements that you're probably already familiar with.

2. **Application (Chapters 2, 4 and 6)**
   In these chapters, you'll learn how to apply the tools you've learned to use. The Application content is progressive; that is, each lesson builds upon all of the tools and techniques that have come before.

3. **Conceptual Corner (Throughout)**
   The Conceptual Corners, which range in length from one to four pages, provide a break from concrete studies of notes and rhythms by exploring some of the more abstract ideas that apply to the art and craft of jazz improvisation. The ideas covered in each Conceptual Corner are applicable to all levels of improvisation, so don't feel obligated to wait until you've worked your way up to the appropriate page to take a look at any of these.

As you use this book, you're encouraged to seek a flexible balance among these three sources of material. To fully grasp an Application lesson, for example, you'll need control of the tools in the corresponding Toolbox; at the same time, those tools need not be practiced only in isolation. The act of applying these tools is itself another useful form of practice. By the same token, most Application techniques can and should be reinforced by practicing them with a variety of tools.

While *The Big Book of Jazz Piano Improvisation* is useful for players with a broad range of skills and experience, from relative neophytes to seasoned pros, some basic background in music is necessary to get the most out of the book. Before you settle in, look through Chapter 1 to make sure that the concepts presented there do not seem brand new or difficult to understand. If you feel you need a more thorough review, check out *Beginning Jazz Keyboard* by Noah Baerman, published by the National Keyboard Workshop/Alfred Publishing.

1

A compact disc is included with this book. Using the CD will help make learning more enjoyable and the information more meaningful. This symbol appears next to every example recorded on the CD. Use the CD to help ensure that you're capturing the feel of the examples, interpreting the rhythms correctly and so on. By adjusting your balance control, you'll be able to hear the rhythm section or click track on its own, so that you can play along. Track 1 includes the note A so that those with electronic keyboards can tune to the CD. Have fun!

INTRODUCTION

Welcome to *The Big Book of Jazz Piano Improvisation*. Here are some important tips to keep in mind as you move forward.

This book is not intended as a textbook in harmony or theory. The study of jazz keyboard is often divided into two areas: harmony (chords) and improvisation (melodic lines). Naturally, you can't get very far in the study of improvisation without a working knowledge of chords and progressions. Some relevant topics are addressed in this book, but you won't find a comprehensive study of harmony. If you're interested in a more in-depth look at harmonic topics, check out *Jazz Keyboard Harmony* by Noah Baerman, published by the National Keyboard Workshop/Alfred Publishing.

Whenever you see an example or sample solo, don't just play it as notated. Think of this as a "do-it-yourself" book. The musical examples are there to help you understand the lessons, but learning them represents only the beginning of your study. The goal is to be able to integrate the ideas you find into your own improvisations, so it's essential that you work and experiment with these ideas in different ways.

Use tunes when you practice. Once you've applied a lesson to a corresponding musical example in the book, there's still much more you can do. A technique that you can use with only one chord progression is of limited use, so you're strongly encouraged to apply everything you learn to a variety of tunes and chord progressions. The examples in this book are based on dozens of progressions that you can use as raw material for improvisation (see page 143 for a complete guide). Check out pages 134–137 for a more in-depth discussion of tunes.

Practice in a variety of tempos. Some progressions and tunes are most typically played either fast ("Giant Steps") or slow ("Body and Soul"), but most jazz tunes work across an entire range of *tempos* (rates of speed). Most of the techniques you learn in this book will be useful at any tempo, so it's important that you practice accordingly.

Practice in all 12 keys. One of the biggest myths in music is that some keys are easy and some are difficult. While certain moves at the keyboard might be easier to execute in one key than in another, the main source of this myth is that any key in which you haven't practiced is automatically difficult. To be truly flexible and to fully integrate any technique or concept, it's important that you practice in all 12 keys. You'll find an overview of how to practice in all 12 keys on page 22 and some additional 12-key material for use with the CD on page 142.

Practice intelligently. Your most important practice strategy is knowing what and how to practice, something you can teach yourself just by being aware. Be sensitive to your strengths and weaknesses and to what you need to work on to take the next step. Be patient with yourself without being complacent. If you sound good every time you practice, you're probably not challenging yourself enough; if each practice session is a demoralizing, overwhelming experience, you're probably challenging yourself too much. Keep close tabs on the progress you're making (or not making), and be flexible in adjusting your practice routine. Also, be sensitive to what your body is telling you; you accomplish nothing by skipping warm-ups or practicing until your arms hurt. You'll accomplish more in an hour of well-thought-out, efficient practice than you will in three hours of poorly planned, inefficient practice.

CONCEPTUAL CORNER I:
SO WHAT IS IMPROVISATION, ANYWAY?

Here we are, still at the very beginning of this book, and guess what: You already know how to improvise. Improvisation, at its heart, is nothing more than the act of creating something in the moment, rather than doing so in a premeditated way. Look at some of the ways that you've probably improvised without even realizing it:

- You're walking down the street. Somebody opens a door right in your path, and you move out of the way. You've shown your ability to improvise a dance; if you were unable to improvise, you would have broken your nose.

- A friend asks how your day went. You give a detailed, descriptive response. You've shown your ability to improvise poetry or prose; if you were unable to improvise, your response would have been either silence or grunting.

- A coworker wants directions to a party you're throwing, but the location is difficult to explain. You take a piece of paper and a pencil and draw a makeshift map. You've shown your ability to improvise visual art; if you were unable to improvise, your coworker would still be driving around, lost.

- A family member comes to you upset by something. You listen to his or her problem and say something comforting, asking questions about the situation. You've shown your ability to improvise a theatrical dialogue; if you were unable to improvise, you would say nothing.

If you've ever encountered and successfully negotiated situations like these, you clearly know how to improvise. The most important aspect of jazz improvisation, or any other kind of improvisation, is the belief in one's basic ability to improvise, to be creative in a spontaneous way. It is a skill that all of us are born with; the key is to recognize it and to trust that it's there when you need it.

So, if you already know how to improvise, how will this book be useful to you? Each of the above situations depends on certain basic skills in addition to the improvisational impulse—for instance, the abilities to read, write and walk. All of these are skills that you've likely mastered and use automatically on a daily basis. At the same time, none of these is purely instinctive; instead, you learned each through study and/or practice, even if you weren't aware of it at the time. Jazz is no different than speaking or writing. It is a way of communicating original, often spontaneous thoughts in a language you've already mastered to some extent: music. In the language of jazz keyboard, as in spoken language, we use vocabulary (notes, rhythms and chords), grammar (specific combinations of notes, rhythms and chords), and a voice (keyboard). Developing fluency in jazz is fundamentally no more mysterious than developing fluency in Swahili, Lithuanian or Finnish. You wouldn't expect to speak any of these languages without learning the grammar, vocabulary and "sound," and you wouldn't expect to become fluent without speaking and studying the language over a period of time. So it goes with jazz, which brings us to the answer to the question posed at the beginning of this paragraph: This book will be useful in helping you learn the language of music as it applies to jazz improvisation.

A typical jazz performance of practically any tune follows a simple format: written melody, improvised solo(s), written melody repeated. Though musicians will tinker with this formula in certain situations, it remains the bread and butter of jazz improvisation. Improvisation fits into this formula in a number of ways and places: introductions and endings can be improvised, chord progressions can be improvised, the phrasing of the written melody can be altered and so on. While we will address possibilities such as these, this book will focus on determining what to play during the improvised solos that come between statements of the melody.

CHAPTER 1 YOUR BASIC TOOLBOX

SCALES

The first thing we'll pull out of our toolbox is *scales.* Most scales in Western music are made up of a specific pattern of *half steps* and *whole steps.* A half step is the shortest distance between two notes. Two half steps make a whole step.

Major Scales

The *major scale,* shown here in the key of C, has the following pattern of half and whole steps. Notice the numbers underneath; these are *degrees,* which show each note's position within the scale.

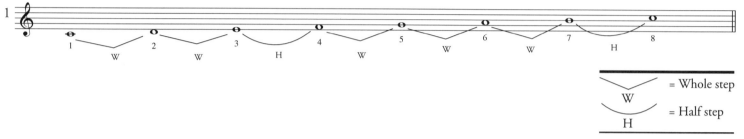

A NOTE ABOUT FINGERING SCALES

Before you actually begin to play the major scales on page 9, it's worth taking a moment to develop some strategies for fingering. Most effective scale fingerings are based on a few basic principles that can be applied to virtually any scale.

- Most traditional scale fingerings are based on the principle of efficiency—that is, minimizing unnecessary motion such as excessive finger crossing. If you cross over (or under) every two notes, you're probably not using the most effective fingering; if you find yourself running out of fingers, you're probably not crossing often enough.

- Avoid using your thumb on black keys. Finger crossing almost always involves the thumb, and if the thumb avoids black keys, the chances of getting tangled are greatly lessened. Most standard fingerings, especially for scales with many black keys, ensure that the thumb always lands on a white key.

- When playing scales, use your 5th finger only on the first note (left hand) or last note (right hand) of the scale. Crossing to or from the 5th finger will land you in an awkward position.

- Look ahead as you play and watch for signposts that suggest fingering strategies. Take note, for example, of how many notes are left in the passage, or how many black keys come before the next white key. Observations like these will help you determine what you need to do to avoid running out of fingers or crossing too often.

- Similar scales often have similar fingerings. Unless it involves a violation of the previous guidelines, you can often apply the fingering for one scale to a different scale that begins on the same note. If you know the fingering for the C Major scale, for example, you can use it for most other seven-note scales that begin on C.

The main principle to keep in mind when it comes to fingering is that using the correct fingers for the job at hand will give you the best results. At the same time, it's important that you stay alert to the unique fingering demands of certain situations. For instance, when scales are used in an improvisation or in the context of a melody, traditional scale fingerings may have to be adjusted accordingly.

Below are all 12 major scales, including their traditional fingerings. Right-hand fingerings are shown above the staff; left-hand fingerings are shown below the staff. Notice that in some instances, two different finger numbers are shown for the same note. Use the number closer to the staff for endings or beginnings of scales, and the other number for scales that continue beyond one octave.

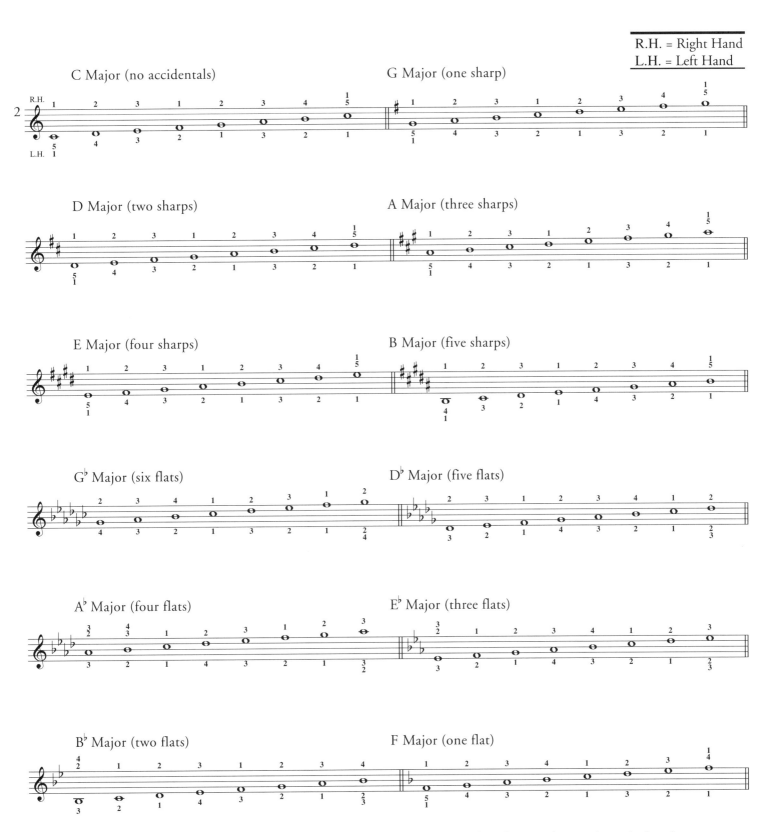

Other scales and keys can be used when *enharmonic equivalents* are employed. An enharmonic equivalent is a note that has a different name but sounds the same. For example, the enharmonic equivalent of G♭ is F♯. So, there can be a key of F♯ which has six sharps (F♯, C♯, G♯, D♯, A♯, E♯). Also, the key of B could be enharmonically respelled as C♭ (seven flats: B♭, E♭, A♭, D♭, G♭, C♭, F♭).

Minor Scales

Minor scale is actually a general reference to several different scale forms. The most basic form of the minor scale is the *natural minor*, which you can think of as a major scale with a lowered 3rd ($\flat$3), lowered 6th ($\flat$6) and lowered 7th ($\flat$7).

Natural Minor Scale

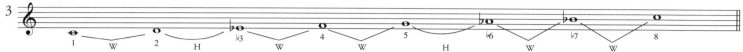

You can think of the *harmonic minor* scale as a major scale with $\flat$3 and $\flat$6. As the name implies, harmonic minor has traditionally been the form of the minor scale from which harmonies are most often derived, though it's also used in melodic contexts.

Harmonic Minor Scale

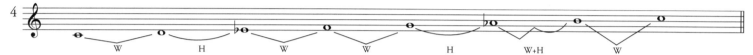

The *melodic minor* scale uses one form when ascending and another when descending. In its ascending form, you can think of melodic minor as a major scale with a $\flat$3. In its descending form, melodic minor is the same as natural minor ($\flat$3, $\flat$6 and $\flat$7). When only the ascending form is used, the scale is often called the *jazz minor* scale.

Melodic Minor Scale

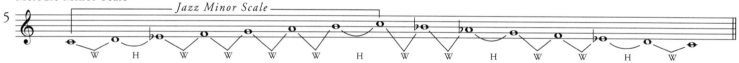

Pentatonic Scales

A *pentatonic scale* is any scale made up of five different notes. Two forms of pentatonic are especially common in jazz. In relation to the major, the *major pentatonic scale* is made up of scale degrees 1, 2, 3, 5 and 6. You can also think of this scale as a major scale with scale degrees 4 and 7 omitted.

The *minor pentatonic scale* is made up of scale degrees 1, $\flat$3, 4, 5 and $\flat$7. It can also be thought of as a natural minor scale with scale degrees 2 and 6 omitted.

Blues Scale

In relation to the major scale, the blues scale is made up of scale degrees 1, $\flat$3, 4, $\flat$5, 5 and $\flat$7. You can also think of the blues scale as a minor pentatonic scale with the addition of $\flat$5.

C Blues

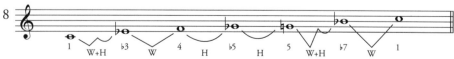

Scale Variations

A number of scales have "alternate" versions that can add color and interest to your improvisations. Example 9 shows two common scale variations.

C Minor Pentatonic (Alternate Version)   C Blues (Alternate Version)

INTERVALS

An *interval* is the measure of distance between two notes. The most basic building blocks for intervals are half steps and whole steps. The intervals we use also have more specific names.

The *class* of an interval is first defined by its size, using a numerical name. For example, to determine the interval class of D up to G, count all the different note names between those two notes (ignoring for now whether they are natural, sharp or flat). In this case, you have D, E, F and G. That's four, so you have some kind of 4th.

The interval's name is then refined by giving it a *quality:* major, minor, perfect, augmented or diminished. The chart below shows the most basic intervals. In addition, any perfect or major interval can be made augmented by making it a half step larger. Any perfect or minor interval can be made diminished by making it a half step smaller. The numerical name can be altered with an accidental to indicate the quality. For example, in C, the second note of the major scale is D, (a major 2nd), which can also be called "2". D♭, a minor second above C, can be called ♭2 ("flat two"); D♯, an augmented 2nd above C, can be called ♯2 ("sharp two").

For each of the intervals below, you're given five pieces of information: the numerical name, the "formal" name, the abbreviation of that name, the size in half steps and an example beginning on the note C.

NUMERICAL NAME	INTERVAL NAME	ABREVIATED NAME	NUMBER OF HALF STEPS	INTERVALS ABOVE MIDDLE C
1	Perfect Unison	PerU	0	
♭2	minor 2nd	min2	1	
2	Major 2nd	Maj2	2	
♭3	minor 3rd	min3	3	
3	Major 3rd	Maj3	4	
4	Perfect 4th	Per4	5	
♯4/♭5 (tritone)	Augmented 4th diminished 5th	Aug4/dim5	6	
5	Perfect 5th	Per5	7	
♯5/♭6	Augmented 5th minor 6th	Aug5/min6	8	
6	Major 6th	Maj6	9	
♭7	minor 7th	min7	10	
7	Major 7th	Maj7	11	
8	Perfect Octave	Per8	12	

KEY SIGNATURES

As you know, the major scale always has the same pattern of whole steps and half steps: W–W–H–W–W–W–H. That's why the major scale always has a certain sound no matter what key it's in. Key signatures tell us which notes in a key have to be raised (with sharps) or lowered (with flats) to retain that sound. These sharps and flats are applied in every octave as long as the key signature is there (and no other accidental, such as a natural sign ♮, has been applied). Sometimes a scale or piece will be minor, not major. If we use the minor key with the same key signature as a major key, we call that the *relative minor*. The relative minor can be found by playing a scale beginning from the 6th degree of its *relative major* scale. For example, if we play a C Major scale starting and ending on A, the 6th degree, we will have A Minor.

C Major/A Minor

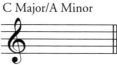

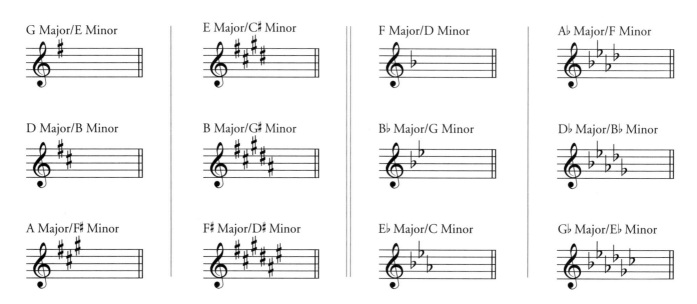

CYCLE OF 5THS

Take a look at the key signatures above. Note that with the sharp keys, every time you move up a 5th, you add a sharp. With the flat keys, every time you move up a 5th, you subtract a flat. This brings us to the *cycle of 5ths*, (the cycle of 4ths if you're moving counterclockwise) or, for the visually inclined, the *circle of 5ths* (or 4ths). This cycle organizes key signatures (or tones) in 5ths. Each key is similar to the key next to it on the circle, with a difference of only one sharp or flat. Major keys are on the outside, minor keys are on the inside.

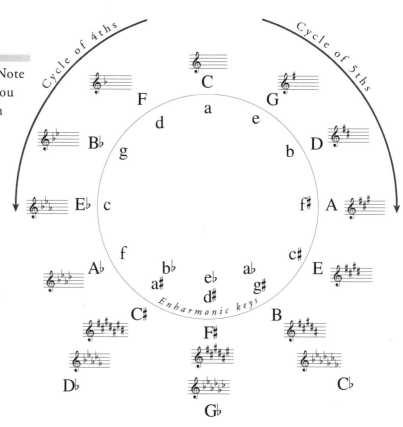

TRIADS

Triads are three-note chords. There are four kinds of triads: *major, minor, augmented* and *diminished*. A triad can be built by using every other note of the first five notes of the major scale. For example, starting on C and selecting every other note of the C Major scale will yield C, E and G—a *C Major triad.* Starting from the lowest note (C) and going up, these notes are called the *root, 3rd* and *5th* of the chord.

C Major Scale   C Major Triad

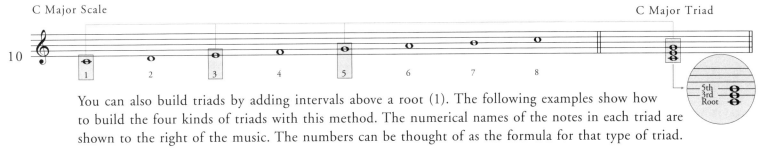

You can also build triads by adding intervals above a root (1). The following examples show how to build the four kinds of triads with this method. The numerical names of the notes in each triad are shown to the right of the music. The numbers can be thought of as the formula for that type of triad.

To build any major triad, we use the note a major 3rd above the root (3) and the note a perfect 5th above the root (5).	

To build a *minor triad*, we lower the 3rd of a major triad (with a flat or a natural sign), leaving the root and 5th the same. This results in a minor 3rd ($^\flat$3) and a perfect 5th (5).	

To build a *diminished triad*, we lower the 5th of a minor triad, resulting in a minor 3rd ($^\flat$3) and a diminished 5th ($^\flat$5).	

To build an *augmented triad*, we raise the 5th of a major triad (using a sharp or a natural sign), resulting in a major 3rd and an augmented 5th (5$^\sharp$).	

This chart shows the abbreviated symbols you may encounter to notate each type of chord. The first symbol listed for each chord is the one that will be used in this book.

TRIAD	POSSIBLE SYMBOLS IN C	FORMULA
Major	C, CMAJ, CM, CΔ	1, 3, 5
Minor	CMIN, CMI, CM, C-	1, $\flat$3, 5
Diminished	CDIM, C°	1, $\flat$3, $\flat$5
Augmented	CAUG, C+	1, 3, $\sharp$5

FOUR-NOTE CHORDS: 7TH AND 6TH CHORDS

While triads are the building blocks of most harmony in the Western world, jazz musicians usually add notes to them, such as 7ths and 6ths, to create other chords. All of the four-note chords below are made by adding a note on top of an existing triad. From the bottom up, the four notes in these chords are called the root, 3rd, 5th and 7th (or 6th, as the case may be).

The *major 7th* chord is made by adding a major 7th above the root of a major triad. It can also be thought of as adding a major 3rd above the 5th of a major triad. The formula is 1, 3, 5, 7.

The *dominant 7th* chord is made by adding a minor 7th above the root of a major triad. It can also be thought of as adding a minor 3rd above the 5th of a major triad. The formula is 1, 3, 5, ♭7.

The *minor 7th* chord is made by adding a minor 7th above the root of a minor triad. It can also be thought of as adding a minor 3rd above the 5th of a minor triad. The formula is 1, ♭3, 5, ♭7.

The *minor 7 flat 5* (or *"half-diminished"*) chord is made by adding a minor 7th above the root of a diminished triad. It can also be thought of as adding a major 3rd above the ♭5 of a diminished triad. The name "half-diminished" means that the 5th is diminished, but not the 7th (as opposed to the "fully diminished" chord below). The formula is 1, ♭3, ♭5, ♭7.

The *diminished 7th* chord is made by adding a diminished 7th above the root of a diminished triad. It can also be thought of as adding a minor 3rd above the ♭5 of a diminished triad. The diminished 7th on top is enharmonically equivalent to a major 6th. The formula is 1, ♭3, ♭5, ♭♭7.

The *major 6th* chord is made by adding a major 6th above the root of a major triad. It can also be thought of as adding a major 2nd above the 5th of a major triad. The formula is 1, 3, 5, 6.

The *minor 6th* chord is made by adding a major 6th above the root of a minor triad. It can also be thought of as adding a major 2nd above the 5th of a minor triad. The formula is 1, ♭3, 5, 6.

The chart below shows the common symbols used for the different types of 7th and 6th chords. As with triads, the first symbol listed for each chord is the one that will be used for the rest of this book.

TRIAD	POSSIBLE SYMBOLS IN C	FORMULA
Major 7	CMAJ7, CM7, C△7	1,3,5,7
Major 6	C6, CMAJ6, CM6, C△6	1,3,5,6
Dominant 7	C7	1,3,5,♭7
Minor 7	CMIN7, CMI7, CM7, C-7	1,♭3,5,♭7
Minor 6	CMIN6, CMI6, CM6, C-6	1,♭3,5,6
Minor 7♭5	CMIN7♭5, Cø, CMI7♭5, CM7♭5, C-7♭5	1,♭3,♭5,♭7
Diminished 7	CDIM7, C°	1,♭3,♭5,♭♭7

Voicings and Inversions

Voicings

A *voicing* is the specific arrangement of notes in a chord. Any chord can be voiced in multiple ways; for example, we can *double* (repeat), add or omit notes. We can choose the order in which to play the notes, where on the keyboard to play the notes, how to get from one chord to the next and so on. When you hear players say "that pianist has great voicings," or "I'm working on Bill Evans and McCoy Tyner voicings," that is what they are talking about.

Inversions

The first step on the road to masterful voicings is the mastery of chord *inversions*. As an example, let's look at a C Major 7th (CMaj7) chord. In its "natural state," with the root on the bottom, it is said to be in *root position*.

If we play the same chord with the 3rd on the bottom, it is in *1st inversion*.

If we play the same chord with the 5th on the bottom, it is in *2nd inversion*.

If we play the same chord with the 7th on the bottom, it is in *3rd inversion*.

Which note you play on the bottom also impacts which note will wind up on top. In a jazz context, we use the top note at least as often as the bottom note in deciding which inversion to use in a given situation. To take it one step further, we can use the concept of inversion as a voicing tool, even with root position chords. If we want to retain the sound of the root on the bottom, but want the flexibility of a different inversion, we can play the inversion of our choice with the right hand and lay down the root underneath with the left hand. In a group setting, we can play the inversion of our choice with either hand and let the bassist play the root.

Root position with 2nd inversion in the right hand.

Diatonic Harmony

Diatonic Harmony in Major Keys

Diatonic means "of the scale," so the most basic definition of *diatonic harmony* is the chords built from a particular scale. While diatonic harmony itself isn't an improvisational tool, any jazz improviser must be able to identify the keys to which the chords in a tune relate, and how those chords function in those keys. One way to build these chords is to stack 3rds on each degree of the scale. In the case of 6th chords, you simply add a 6th above the root. (Note that in improvisational situations, 6th chords are often used in place of Maj7 chords.) Below are the diatonic 7th chords in the key of C. Note the use of Roman numerals under the music. They are discussed below.

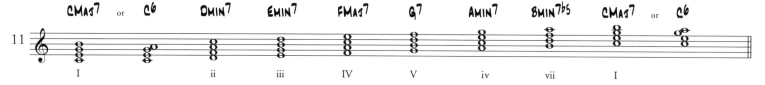

We use Roman numerals to signify the scale degree a chord is built on, since they're not specific to a particular key. We use uppercase Roman numerals for chords with a major 3rd (major, augmented, major 6, major 7 and dominant 7), and lowercase for those with a minor 3rd (minor, diminished, minor 7, minor 6, minor 7 flat five and diminished 7). Here's a quick review of the Roman numerals you'll need and their Arabic equivalents:

Roman Numeral	Arabic Equivalant
I ...... or ...... i 1	
II ...... or ...... ii 2	
III ..... or ...... iii 3	
IV ...... or ...... iv 4	
V .... or ...... v 5	
VI ...... or ...... vi 6	
VII .... or ...... vii 7	

Notation using Roman numerals is useful because the kind of chord built on each degree is the same in every key. Here are the diatonic 7 chords that you'll find in every major key:

Degree	Quality
I	Maj7/6
ii	min7
iii	min7
IV	Maj7
V	Dom7
vi	min7
vii	min7♭5

As a tool for memorizing the diatonic chords in every key, make yourself a chart like this:

Key	I	ii	iii	IV	V	vi	vii
C	CMaj7	Dmin7	Emin7	FMaj7	G7	Amin7	Bmin7♭5
G	GMaj7	Amin7	Bmin7	CMaj7	D7	Emin7	F♯min7♭5
Continue through all the keys in the cycle of 5ths.							

Diatonic Harmony in Minor Keys

The most obvious way to find the diatonic 7th chords in a minor key is to look at the relative major key, borrow the chords and shift the Roman numerals. Here are the diatonic 7th chords for A Minor, the relative minor of C Major:

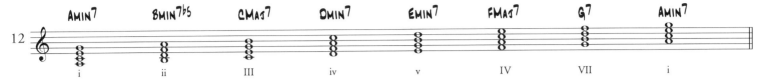

It doesn't end there, however. What you see above is based on the natural minor scale. But as we know, the natural minor is only one of three types of minor scales (see page 10). The primary use of the harmonic minor scale is just as the name implies—it's a scale from which harmonies are derived. This is because it provides a dominant 7 chord on V. Here are diatonic 7 chords of an A Harmonic Minor scale:

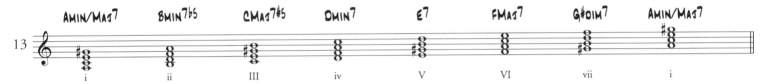

As we can see, the i chord in harmonic minor is a minor chord with a major 7th (min/Maj7 or min♮7) and the III chord is a major 7 chord with a raised 5th (Maj7♯5). These are both unusual chords that sound most appropriate in a very modern setting. We'll examine both of these chords later as we explore modern and non-diatonic harmony.

In real musical situations, chords from both the natural and harmonic minor scales are used side by side—most often, i and III from natural minor, V and vii from harmonic minor, and the ii, iv and VI common to both. Sometimes, a min6 chord is used in place of the min7 i chord.

Chord Changes and the ii–V–I Progression

Using Roman numerals, we can identify the common ways in which chords move from one to the next. In jazz, these specific combinations of chords, or *progressions,* are most often referred to as *chord changes* or simply *changes.* The progression that serves as the backbone for the majority of jazz tunes is the famous ii–V–I (ii–V–i in minor).

Most music builds excitement (*tension*) and then gives the listener some closure (*resolution*). The study of jazz chord progressions is really a study of how to build up different amounts of tension and how to achieve different levels of resolution. The dominant chord resolving to the I or i chord a perfect 5th below is the essence of tension and resolution in Western harmony. Play this and hear for yourself how this works in both major and minor keys.

The next step is the ii chord. Since our ears are used to the sound of one chord moving to another chord a 5th below, as in example 16, we can precede the V chord with the chord a 5th above—the ii chord. However, the dominant 7 chord that serves as the V in both major and minor keys has an unstable sound that wants to resolve—that's why it sounds so good when it resolves to the I chord. By going from ii to V, you actually prolong and intensify the tension, which in turn makes the resolution more dramatic.

Voice Leading

If you've spent any time with harmony, you've surely dealt with *voice leading* on some level. Voice leading is the smooth movement of the notes (or *voices*) from one chord to the next, and it applies to any type of voicing. The whole idea comes from vocal groups. If you have four voice parts in a choir, the goal is to create rich-sounding chords with those four voices. Just as important, though, is that each voice in the choir has smooth, singable lines, rather than a sequence of acrobatic leaps. Good voice leading bridges the gap between these two goals. Compare the voice leading in examples 18A and 18B.

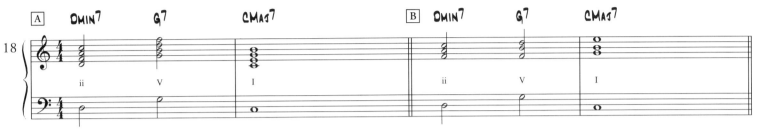

If you follow any individual voice in the first two bars, you'll find a series of leaps that would be difficult to sing. Although at the keyboard you don't need to literally sing the lines, the result of this leaping is that the chords don't sound as if they relate to one another. Even though it uses the same basic chords, the second example sounds more like a "natural" progression because of the voice leading that allows for smooth movement between voices.

A basic technique for getting started with voice leading is to calculate the shortest distance each voice can move to arrive at the next chord. In other words, you must figure out which appropriate voicing for the following chord will involve the least movement.

Note that the roots played by the left hand are not expected to follow the guidelines of smooth voice leading. In fact, it is the leaping movement of the roots that clarifies the harmonic movement in the smoothly changing chord voicings above.

Having a solid grasp of voice leading is useful beyond helping you play chords smoothly. Since chords often form the basis for improvised solo lines, mastery of voice leading is crucial in developing fluency as a soloist. When you practice, work on being able to lead any voice in a chord to a nearby voice in the next chord.

LEAD SHEETS

Lead sheets are probably the most common way of notating jazz tunes or other songs that are to be played in a jazz setting. In contrast to fully notated music, a lead sheet provides you with the bare-bones musical information—melody, chords and form—that you need to play a tune. This allows for a creative, personal interpretation and gives you a jumping-off place for improvisation.

You'll often encounter lead sheets in the context of a *fake book* or *real book,* which is essentially a single-volume collection of lead sheets for different tunes. (In case you're wondering: Despite the name, some fake books are considered a "legit" source of tunes.)

Example 20 uses lead sheet–style notation for a jazzed-up version of the old classic "Greensleeves." This tune has been recorded by many jazz artists, including John Coltrane, Jimmy Smith, Ben Webster, Coleman Hawkins, Oscar Peterson and Ray Bryant.

Greensleeves

HARMONIC ANALYSIS

Harmonic analysis involves the identification of chords and patterns of chords within a set of changes. Harmonic analysis is useful in a number of ways. Being able to improvise in a key depends on knowing what key you're in at any given moment. Harmonic analysis is also a great way to simplify harmonic information. The easier it is to categorize a progression and its component parts, the easier it is to remember and make use of that progression. And, since many progressions in jazz harmony appear again and again, the ability to quickly and accurately identify these common progressions will give you much more fluency as an improviser.

Harmonic analysis begins with identifying the key involved and the functions of the chords (expressed as Roman numerals) as they relate to that key.

If you can process and understand the above progression as "iii–vi–ii–V–I in C," you've grasped the basics of harmonic analysis. Harmonic analysis can be fairly easy, provided that you have a solid understanding of the diatonic chords in every key (which you learned about on page 16). Because the ii–V–I progression is so common, it's especially important that you're comfortable with the chords involved in this progression in every key. Hunting down this progression, in fact, is a useful way to determine what key a tune is in at any given moment. A good approach to harmonic analysis is to first look for V–I and ii–V–I in the music, and then work backward to trace the harmonic path that brought you to that point.

Modulation

Since few jazz tunes stay in a single key from beginning to end, a thorough knowledge of the diatonic chords in every key is essential. Most tunes contain at least one *modulation*, or change of key. Your knowledge of diatonic chords will help you recognize that you've moved from one key to another, and will also help you identity the chords used in the new key. Example 22 modulates from C Major to E♭ Minor.

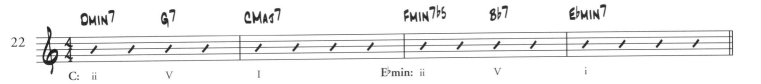

If the exact point at which a tune moves from key to another is unclear, a *pivot chord* may be involved. A pivot chord is a chord that functions in both keys in a modulation, providing a seamless transition between the two. If a chord or series of chords fits this description, you get to choose which key to think about when you get there. Notice the dual function of the pivot chord in example 23.

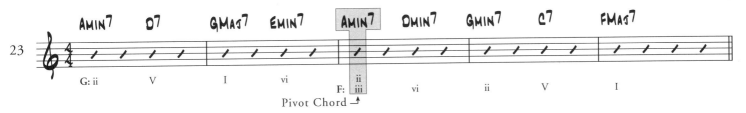

When doing harmonic analyses, you may sometimes encounter chords that don't seem to make sense. Chances are, these chords simply relate to a harmonic concept you haven't yet learned. Not to worry; make note of these chords, and as you continue to develop your harmonic chops, go back to them and see if you can figure out how they function.

PLAYING IN ALL 12 KEYS —TRANSPOSITION

The most basic definition of *transposition* is playing music in a key other than the one in which it was written. Throughout this book, you'll find references to practicing examples (which may include progressions, melodies or both) in all 12 keys. Fluency in harmonic analysis is very helpful in transposing chord progressions, since it boils down to simple math. Look at the first three measures of example 24. The harmonic formula for these measures is basically ii–V–I in the home key (G) followed by V–I in the key a major 2nd lower (F). To transpose this example, you simply need to retain this chord-to-chord relationship in whatever new key you choose, using the ii chord in the new key as your starting point. Measures 4–6 show this example transposed to C Major. Notice that the chord types (Maj7, min7, etc.) and harmonic relationships are exactly the same as those in the original key.

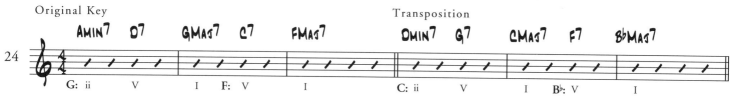

You can also think in terms of moving each chord up or down by the same exact interval (in the example above, a perfect 4th higher or a perfect 5th lower), though this hunt-and-peck approach tends to be slower, and it obscures the overall harmonic shape.

When it comes to transposing melodies, the note-at-a-time approach is even more cumbersome, especially when a phrase is dense with notes. Have no fear: There are a number ways to easily and functionally transpose a melodic line. The first way is to think in a horizontal or linear fashion. To transpose a line horizontally, first determine the key or scale and assign the corresponding scale degree to each note. Then, simply apply this sequence of scale degrees to whatever key or scale you choose.

Another way to transpose melodies is to use a vertical or chord-related approach. In this approach, the notes of the melody are related directly to the underlying chords. Naturally, this approach is particularly useful for melodies that use *arpeggios* (chords played one note at a time) or similar devices. Relate each note in the melody to the chord occurring at that moment, and transpose accordingly. In the scale degrees written below the music, notes not belonging to the chord are in parentheses.

In all instances, you're strongly encouraged to supplement the process of transposition with the actual sound. In other words, make sure you can *hear* as well as understand the transposition. Any attempt at transposition will be more effective if your ears take an active role in the process.

CHAPTER 2   APPLICATION OF BASIC TOOLS

TWO AND FOUR: THE BACKBEAT

When digging into jazz improvisation, having a good and authentic *feel* is of utmost importance. While feel comes mostly from prolonged exposure to good, swingin' jazz, there are some tangible elements you can keep in mind and work on. One of these is the *backbeat*, a rhythmic emphasis on beats 2 and 4 in a measure of $\frac{4}{4}$. In most rock and blues music, the backbeat is played in a very obvious fashion on the snare drum. When playing jazz with a swing feel, the backbeat is often far less explicit, but it's invariably felt by all the musicians as the heartbeat of the music.

The next time you hear a swingin' jazz group play, check out the band member in charge of counting off the tunes. You're likely to find that the feel and tempo of the tune is established by snapping the fingers on beats 2 and 4. As the musicians play, you may notice one or more of them keeping time by tapping their feet on beats 2 and 4.

It's never too soon to get used to feeling the backbeat. One way to get started is to choose a fairly simple song or passage that you feel comfortable with. Play the melody with the right hand while snapping beats 2 and 4 with the fingers of your left. Or, play the melody with one or both hands, and tap your foot on beats 2 and 4.

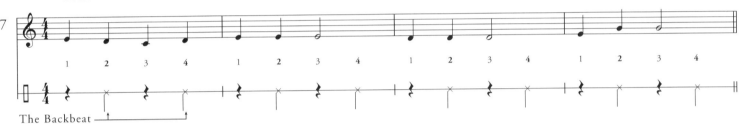

It's also helpful (and common among jazz musicians) to use a metronome to reinforce the backbeat. Set the metronome at half your chosen tempo, and use the clicks as beats 2 and 4.

Swing Eighths

Unless otherwise noted, the examples throughout this book are to be played with *swing eighths*. Swing eighths involve pairs of eighth notes in which the first note (or rest) is longer than the second. Though swing feel is hard to define, and even harder to notate, swing eighths are often approximated as eighth-note triplets in which the first two eighths are tied together

Compared to swing eighths, straight eighths are usually too stiff for swingin' jazz, while dotted eighth/sixteenth pairs tend to sound too bouncy and a bit hokey.

SYNCOPATION

The most basic definition of *syncopation* is the accenting of weak beats or weak parts of beats. Syncopation is critical to the rhythmic identity of jazz. In jazz, syncopation usually occurs on *offbeats* (the "and" count, or second half, of each beat). Play the straight (that is, syncopation-free) melody below. Notice that the accents naturally fall directly on the beats.

The two melodies in example 31, on the other hand, contain a great deal of syncopation. This time, the accents fall on the offbeats, while rests, unaccented notes or tied-over notes fall directly on the beats.

When it comes to playing jazz, it's essential that you're comfortable with syncopation. This entails being able not only to play the syncopated rhythms, but also to keep track of where the beats are. The amount of syncopation in a tune or improvised solo can vary greatly from just a few instances of syncopation to syncopation throughout, or anything in between.

Anticipation

A special form of syncopation is *anticipation*, in which a note is played before the "target" beat. In most cases, anticipations occur on the beat or offbeat immediately preceding the target beat. Anticipations are particularly noticeable when they occur at the bar line or over a change of chord. Compare the first, completely unsyncopated melody in example 32A to the melody in example 32B, which uses anticipations (highlighted in gray).

Anticipation highlighted

Note that in almost all cases involving anticipations, the chord symbols appear over the target beats. This practice not only reinforces the location of downbeats, but also takes into account that anticipations are generally not essential to the song's structure.

CONCEPTUAL CORNER:
EAR TRAINING

A jazz musician with undeveloped ears is like a cook who uses only salt and pepper to flavor food: The results may be functional, but are unlikely to be soulful or interesting. No aspect of jazz can be mastered without the ability to hear it, so it's time to grab your ear barbells and get to work! First, we'll look at some particular areas, then we'll explore some suggestions for practice and mastery.

What Should Your Ears Be Trained to Do?

Identify intervals. Intervals (see page 11) are the building blocks of chords and melodic lines, so the ability to accurately hear them will go a long way toward sharpening your musical hearing. Along those lines, the ability to hear intervals is the key to developing good *relative pitch* (the ability to identify different pitches, intervals and chords in relation to one another). Relative pitch is absolutely essential for jazz musicians. You should develop your skills to the point you can identify any interval, *harmonically* (pitches sounding simultaneously) or melodically (one note at a time), ascending or descending.

Decipher rhythms. Because so much jazz is dependent upon rhythm, it's essential that you become fluent in hearing and identifying rhythms and rhythmic patterns. If you hear a rhythm, you should be able to recreate and transcribe it (show it in standard notation).

Figure out melodic lines. Once you have a good grasp of intervals and rhythms, melodies are the next step. You should be able to put these elements together to identify both the pitches and rhythms in a melody. This topic is discussed further on pages 39–41.

Identify chords and progressions. Your ability to hear intervals will also serve you well as you learn to hear chords, since every chord is made up of intervals. The stage of learning you've reached at any point will determine the complexity of the chords you're able to identify by sound. Begin with root-position triads, move on to 7th chords, and then add other elements to the mix—different inversions and voicings, altered notes, and so on). You should also develop the ability to identify chord progressions, through the movement of the roots (itself a melody within the progression) and familiar, recognizable patterns (such as ii–V–I).

Sight-sing. Sight-singing, the ability to sing an unfamiliar melody directly from the page, is useful for understanding a new melody before you actually play it. More importantly, it's a great way to test how clearly you can hear intervals, rhythms and entire melodies in your head without relying on an instrument.

Hear a melodic line in your head before you play it. This principle is similar to sight-singing, in this case applied to improvisation. In other words, before you play a line, you should first be able to hear it in your head. If you can't do this, it could mean that the line you're about to play may be comfortable under your fingers, but may not truly be a product of your creativity.

How Do You Train Your Ear to Do These Things?

Work with recorded examples. Many products are designed expressly to help you develop the skills we looked at above. Drills for each type of practice can be found on commercially produced sound and video recordings and software. Do some research first to ensure that you get a product compatible with your skill level and the specific aspects of ear training you want to improve. You can even make your own practice recordings that focus on the areas and types of exercises that work best for you.

Work with other people. The best and most interactive option is to find a practice partner or a study group. This way, you can tailor a routine to your specific needs and get feedback from other musicians.

Play things for yourself. Playing the sounds (intervals, chords, progressions, etc.) that you want to familiarize yourself with offers a very personalized way to develop fluency in identifying these sounds.

Use recorded music. Learning to hear and identify specific intervals, chords and progression from a recording can be one of the most practical, stimulating and relevant workouts for your ears. We'll explore this idea in further detail on pages 39–41.

Soloing Basics: Chord Tones

Chord Tones as Arpeggios

As we begin to explore the question of which notes to play when improvising a solo, the most obvious choice is to play *chord tones*—the notes used in the underlying chords. One advantage to using chord tones is the assurance that your improvised melody will relate to the harmony. Chord tones can be played as either *block chords* (all notes played at once) or as arpeggios. You'll find arpeggios a useful device for improvising melodies.

When practicing a set of changes, anything from a simple ii–V–I to an entire tune, being able to arpeggiate all the chords in the progression is a terrific jumping-off point. Example 34 shows arpeggios over a set of changes in the style of the A section of "Time Was," a standard recorded by John Coltrane, Bud Powell, Kenny Barron and others.

On page 19, we looked at voice leading as a way of smoothing out the movement from chord to chord. Example 35 uses the same changes as those in example 34, here arpeggiated with smooth voice leading from each chord to the next.

You're encouraged to practice all progressions in this way—arpeggiating the chords, connecting each to the next as smoothly as possible.

Another way to practice and use arpeggios is to change the order of the notes. The examples on page 26 all moved up through an arpeggio and back down again on the same chord or the next. Example 36 shows some ways to vary the direction of the arpeggios. On page 37, we'll explore the idea of melodic contour in greater depth. Note that while there is increased variety in the order of the notes, smooth voice leading is present throughout.

Chord Tones and Rhythm

Having developed the flexibility and technical fluency to use arpeggios in the different ways we've explored, the next step is to vary the rhythm. Instead of a constant stream of eighth notes, example 37 uses some different rhythmic possibilities, including syncopation and anticipation. If you like, peek ahead to page 35 for a more thorough exploration of rhythmic variety.

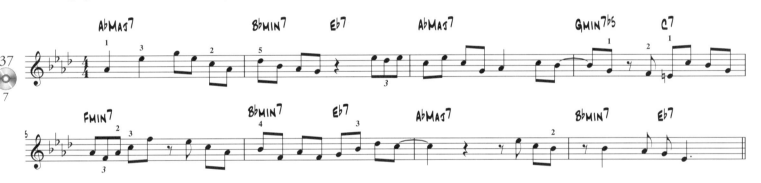

While any of the chord-tone techniques we've been exploring can be used in an improvised solo, they provide their greatest benefit as practice tools. Just as musicians practice scales without expecting to perform them at a recital, jazz musicians practice arpeggios over chord progressions in various ways. The result is a mastery of chord tones for use in any improvisation. Example 38 shows one possibility.

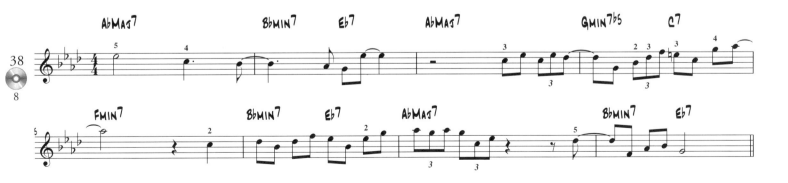

MAJOR SCALE OPTIONS

Having explored the ways that you can solo using chord tones, we'll now take a different approach. Another way to choose the notes for an improvisation or solo is to use scales that relate to the key you're in at any moment. The first step is to determine the key of the tune or, when applicable, the keys through which the tune modulates. For a major key, you can solo by choosing your notes from the corresponding major scale. To practice this method, play the major scale in the appropriate key(s) while playing the chords, as demonstrated in example 39. The changes are in the style of those used in the opening eight bars of Eddie "Cleanhead" Vinson's "Tune-Up," a tune associated with Miles Davis and recorded by many others, including Max Roach, Wes Montgomery and Sonny Rollins.

Another option in a major key is to use the major pentatonic scale. In some cases, because of its simplicity, this scale may actually be preferable to the major scale, while in other cases that simplicity can be limiting. Over time, you'll learn to choose wisely. Example 40 below uses the changes from example 39.

In performance, there are many ways to add color and variety to these scales. As with arpeggios, you can vary the rhythms and the order of the notes. You can also mix and match, using both the major and minor pentatonic scales at different times rather than using only one throughout.

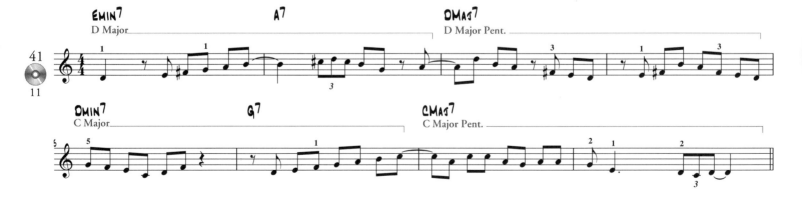

Minor Scale Options

With minor keys, you can use basically the same approach that you use for major keys—that is, determine which key you're in, choose the appropriate scale or scales to use as the basis for your improvisation, and practice the scale(s) with the chords.

Minor-key harmonies in jazz tunes are usually based on a combination of chords derived from the natural and harmonic minor scales. Therefore, it's helpful to pay attention to which form of the scale matches up well with different chords. Unless you're going for a deliberately angular sound, which we'll explore later in the book, the natural minor scale works best with most chords in a minor key. However, the harmonic minor is better suited to use with the dominant 7. You can also apply the harmonic minor to ii–V in a minor key, as long as you take care to return to the natural minor with the return of i. The changes in examples 42–44 are in the style of the first eight bars of Kenny Dorham's "Blue Bossa," a jazz standard popularized by Joe Henderson and recorded by many artists, including pianists McCoy Tyner, Tommy Flanagan, Michel Camilo and Chick Corea. Play the examples on this page with straight eighths, and aim for creating a Latin feeling.

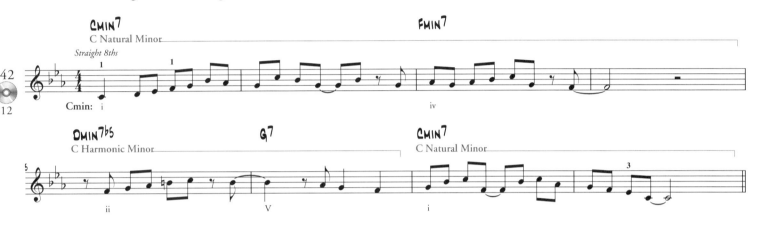

As was the case with the major pentatonic scale on page 28, the minor pentatonic scale offers a simpler sound than that of the different forms of the minor scale, while the ♭5 of the blues scale will add a little extra color to your improvisations. Because of the scale's earthy sound, the ear forgives the occasional *dissonances* (clashing sounds) that sometimes result.

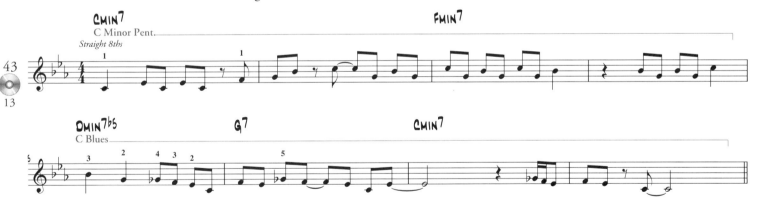

Once you're fluent with all of these scales, try combining them in a single solo.

Using the Melody: Embellishment and Paraphrase

Let's start this discussion with the following statement: "I like salad." To *embellish* this statement, you would begin with the essence of the statement and then add descriptive or colorful details. You might say, "I like salad with lettuce and carrots," or "Hoo-wee, I sure do dig me some salad!" To *paraphrase* this statement, you would try to capture the statement's essence and content using different words. For example, you might say, "I enjoy salad" or "Salad pleases me." Paraphrase and embellishment are both key to making language colorful and flexible.

The concepts of embellishment and paraphrase can be directly translated to melodic improvisation. From a technical standpoint, both paraphrase and embellishment are approached in the same way—that is, using various techniques to alter an existing melody. The main difference between the two lies in how and where to use each.

Embellishment is typically used for the initial or closing statement of a written melody. It's a common tool, though one to be used with caution. For example, if you're playing the melody in unison with another musician, embellishment is usually less appropriate unless it's preplanned. It's also usually most appropriate to embellish the melody in such a way that it's still recognizable. What constitutes recognizable is often a fine line, so it's important to use your most considered musical judgment.

Paraphrase typically takes place during the improvised solo by incorporating the sound of the written melody into your improvisational ideas. A paraphrase functions both as a source of content and a way to achieve continuity within a performance of a song. In this case, there is much less responsibility to be true to the original melody.

For a demonstration of how to alter a melody, let's begin with the standard "Billy Boy." This folk tune was jazzed up by Ahmad Jamal in the early 1950s and was a hit later in the decade for Red Garland. Many other pianists—including Oscar Peterson, Hampton Hawes, Ramsey Lewis and Benny Green—recorded "Billy Boy," so it's a good tune for comparative study. Example 45 shows the basic melody for the first eight bars, with the standard jazz changes.

Now, let's take a look at some of the techniques that are useful for embellishment and paraphrase.

Subtraction

In this technique, which in some ways is the opposite of embellishment, you condense the melody by eliminating some of the notes. When using this technique, be sure that the elimination of notes doesn't obscure the original melody. Take a look at example 46, a "subtracted" version of example 45, noting how the subtraction of certain notes (here, replaced with rests or larger note values) changes the character of the passage.

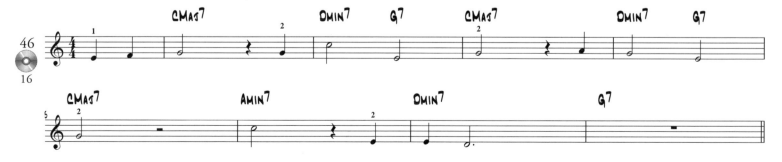

Addition

In this technique, you decorate the existing melody by adding notes to it. Which notes you can or should add is a personal choice, based on the musical vocabulary you've amassed and your sensitivity to the style of the music. If you proceed with care, you can even sometimes use "added" notes to replace notes in the melody.

Altered Rhythms

This technique is fairly self-explanatory: You keep the original pitches, but change the rhythms. As with the previous techniques, you should be sensitive to how your rhythmic alterations impact the melody and reflect the style of the music.

All of the Above

To attain the highest level of mastery, it's useful to practice each of the preceding techniques separately. That said, most successful embellishments and paraphrases of existing melodies depend on combining the techniques for the utmost variety and color. Example 49 uses addition, subtraction and altered rhythms.

All of these techniques are useful in improvisation, regardless of your skill level. As your skills increase, so too will your sophistication in applying these techniques. At the same time, your growth will invariably make embellishment and paraphrase more and more intuitive over time. Ideally, neither embellishment nor paraphrase should be a technical or intellectual process, but rather a spontaneous and sincere means of expression. These tools can enable you to explore and express your relationship to a melody at any moment. However you choose to use these tools, remember that it is crucial to first know the existing melody well.

Patterns

In jazz, a *pattern* is a short melodic phrase composed of a distinctive set of intervals which can be repeated and varied. For example, look at the simple pattern at right—four ascending stepwise notes. Planting this simple seed can help germinate a wealth of material. Example 50 uses the same pattern as a way of moving up the C Major scale.

Example 51 uses the same pattern as a way of descending through the C Major scale.

Example 52 applies the pattern to the C Natural Minor scale.

Example 53 applies the pattern to the C Major Pentatonic scale. Notice the melodic skips and different number of measures that result.

As you can see, even a single, simple pattern can generate all sorts of possibilities. As you learn more scales and chords, your options for any given pattern will naturally increase. You can even create a rudimentary melody by applying a single pattern to each change of chord. Check out example 54, in which a simple arpeggio pattern outlines a iii–vi–ii–V–I progression.

Here are some tips and observations for practicing patterns:

- Practicing patterns is a great technique builder.
- Practicing scales with patterns will allow you to dig in deeper than just playing them straight up and down.
- Repetition is a very effective way of reinforcing an idea.
- Repetition, especially with subtle variations, is a very effective way of reinforcing an idea.
- Repetition…well, you get the picture. Take a look at the next page for more on using patterns.

CREATING YOUR OWN PATTERNS

There are a number of interesting sources for melodic patterns that you may find useful as a point of departure. For example, much of C. L. Hanon's famous book *The Virtuoso Pianist* consists of simple melodic patterns strung together into technique building exercises. Musicologist Nicolas Slonimsky and wind player Yusef Lateef compiled exhaustive and highly praised books of scales and melodic patterns. These sources alone could keep any musician busy for years. However, virtually any melodic line can be transformed into a melodic pattern. There are also several ways to transform a melody or pattern to create even more options. As an example, let's look at the French folk tune "Frère Jacques."

Let's use measure 1 as the basis for a pattern. Here's the same sequence of notes, with note values cut in half, played through an ascending C Major scale.

As cool as it is that we were able to swipe a pattern from such a simple tune, we don't have to stop there. One way we can modify the pattern is through *inversion*—in this context, playing the pattern upside down. In a sense, inversion creates a mirror image of the original melody; where the original melody goes up, the inversion will go down, and vice versa. Here's our pattern inverted and played through an ascending C Major scale:

Another way to alter a pattern is through *retrograde*—playing the pattern backward (from end to beginning). Begin with the last note in the pattern, and work backward to the first. Here's our pattern in retrograde, again played through an ascending C Major scale.

Here's the pattern used with a combination of retrograde and inversion, usually called—surprise—*retrograde inversion.*

INCORPORATING PATTERNS INTO A SOLO

Now that we've begun to explore patterns, how do we actually use them in an improvisation? The first step is to determine the keys involved. The next step is to choose a pattern and a scale that works with that pattern. Then, you'll need to practice playing the pattern up and down through the appropriate scale(s). Example 60 uses the "Frère Jacques" pattern we looked at on page 33. The changes are in the style of those used at the beginning of the popular standard "How High the Moon" and in Little Bennie Harris's bebop classic "Ornithology."

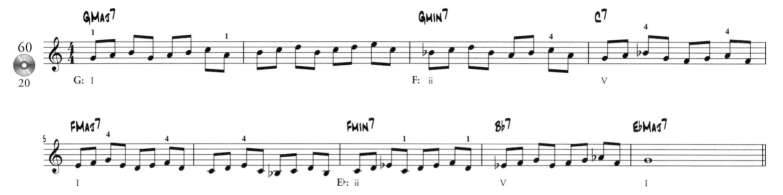

Once you're comfortable with example 60, try adding some variety to the rhythm.

The next step is to use patterns as only one of a number of improvisational tools. In other words, it's time to incorporate other soloing elements before the patterns wear out their welcome. Example 62 alternates between patterns and arpeggios.

Keep in mind that patterns played "straight" can easily sound mechanical. Finding ways to add variety and musicality to patterns is key to taking them out of the practice room and being able to use them naturally within an improvised solo on a tune.

RHYTHMIC VARIETY

Rhythm is central to jazz, and certain elements of jazz rhythm are especially characteristic. We've already discussed swing eighths, the backbeat and syncopation. Still, all of these can become irrelevant if your playing lacks sufficient variety. Play example 60 and imagine how it might sound as an improvised solo.

Not a bad melody, but pretty boring. Try changing the rhythms and other aspects of the melody to give it a little more motion.

Still pretty dull; after all, every note falls right on a beat. How about a swing-eighth rhythm?

Not bad, but still dull. Try using triplets and a melodic pattern.

Swingin' jazz has to have syncopation. Try adding it to this melody.

By now, you can probably see that any of these options can quickly become boring if used without variety. However, combining these elements with taste and skill will keep listeners on their toes and make each subtle change in rhythm that much more exciting and meaningful. Use a variety of note lengths, rhythmic techniques such as syncopation, rests and so on to help foster this excitement.

Example 69 demonstrates a varied use of the possibilities we looked at on page 35. The changes are in the style of the standard "Autumn Leaves," which has been played and recorded countless times. Some of the more influential versions include those by Ahmad Jamal, Bill Evans, Erroll Garner, Keith Jarrett and Cannonball Adderley with Miles Davis. Notice that the notes of the melody are all chord tones, which will make it easier to focus on the rhythms. Pay particular attention to the ways in which the rhythm is varied, and work on incorporating that sort of variety into your own improvisation according to your own tastes and ability.

MELODIC CONTOUR

The *contour* of an object refers to its shape or form. The idea of contour can be applied as well to a melodic line, which also has a shape determined by the movement of the pitches. A melodic line may move up or down; it may move in a completely stepwise fashion, or it may be full of leaps; those leaps may be small, or they may be large. As you might expect, a more interesting contour can make for a more interesting melodic line.

In fact, along with rhythmic variety, contour is one of the key elements in developing a convincing jazz sound. You can be a master of scales, arpeggios and even rhythm, but without a good feeling for contour, your lines will sound like technical exercises. On the other hand, good rhythm and strong contours can make even the most unlikely note choices sound convincing. Whether aware of it or not, any listener can tell the difference between a developed, well-balanced contour and a haphazard one. The need for good contour in music is much like the need for contour in speech. If you've ever heard someone speak in a monotone, you know that the rise and fall of a voice makes speech stimulating and expressive. The results can be subtle or dramatic, but without contour, even the most meaningful spoken words become stupefying.

Cultivating variety in the movement of your melodies is the key element in creating an effective melodic contour. Even with rhythmic variety, a melodic line that moves straight up or down a scale, as in example 70, can become monotonous.

Likewise, a series of skips in the same direction (such as an arpeggio) tends to get old fast when presented without variety.

Combining some of these elements can help improve a contour. For example, you could move both up and down a scale within a single melodic line. At the same time, notice that while this is of some help in example 72, it doesn't quite make for a compelling melodic line in itself.

Enough about why contours can sound bad; let's talk about how to make them sound good. Many of the principles we use in creating jazz melodies can be traced back to *Gradus ad Parnassum*, a 1725 treatise on the study and rules of counterpoint by Johann Fux. While playing a swingin' jazz solo is a few degrees removed from creating a proper *cantus firmus* (a fixed melody traditionally used as the basis for creating counterpoint), the essence of what Fux had to say in regard to contour is still applicable. Above all, try to limit the amount of stepwise movement in the same direction. If you've been moving stepwise in the same direction for a while, it's a good time to break things up with a leap in the opposite direction.

Along the same lines, leaps (especially large leaps) can be counterbalanced with stepwise motion in the opposite direction. In fact, the larger the leap, the greater the need to provide this balance in the contour.

From these examples, you may have deduced that the basic principle behind these guidelines is contrast. Just as we discovered when examining rhythm, too much of any one thing will ultimately become monotonous. Ascending, descending, stepwise motion, small leaps, large leaps: All of these need to be mixed up to achieve a satisfying variety. This doesn't mean that you're forbidden to stick with one thing for a while. However, you should be aware that the longer you stay with any one thing, the greater the need becomes to do something dramatically different to provide contrast.

Example 75 demonstrates the combination of different types of motion into an effective melodic contour. The changes are in the style of the Gershwin standard "Summertime," which has been recorded countless times, including classic versions by Sidney Bechet, John Coltrane and Gil Evans (both with and without Miles Davis).

CONCEPTUAL CORNER:
TRANSCRIPTION

One of the most valuable educational tools we have at all levels of jazz studies is transcription. For some people, the idea of transcribing brings up images of 1950s businessman bellowing, "Marge, take a letter..." as his secretary scrambles to write down the words he dictates. Musical transcription involves the same concept—capturing sounds and recording them in some way. The difference here is that we are capturing musical notes rather than words.

Why transcribe music? The very act of learning jazz requires some knowledge of how others have approached certain musical situations. We all have moments when we hear something that speaks to us in some way and we want to deepen our understanding of what it is. Transcribing the sounds in question can give us access to information directly from the source. Our goal is not to regurgitate the language of other players, but to learn from that language, a learning process that no jazz musician can avoid.

Even if someone else has already transcribed that Bud Powell lick that you've been checking out (many books of transcriptions are available), it is still often more beneficial to do it yourself, as the process will ensure that you dig deeper into the sound. Transcription is one of the best means of ear training that any jazz musician can use. It challenges you, and unlike more mechanical ear training drills, you will have also learned something else by the time you've finished.

Virtually all transcription relies on using a recording of some sort as the source material. Theoretically, you could transcribe something as it was being played live, but without a photographic memory, it's seldom possible to capture anything aside from isolated fragments in this manner. There are many different ways to use recordings for transcription. Each method has a different function and requires different materials and skills.

What to Transcribe

Solos
One of the most common uses of transcription (and one of the most relevant to this book) is learning or "decoding" great solos. The solos may be for piano, organ or other keyboard instrument, or they may be played by another instrument entirely. However, if the solo we love is played by a trumpet, saxophone or guitar, we are still entitled as keyboardists to transcribe it. And, the solo needn't be the most exceptional solo in the world. If you like it, that's justification enough. If you're fond of a particular player, you needn't find the best solo that he or she ever recorded. Find one that sounds good and get to work—or better yet, pick a few of them. That way, you'll learn which elements are consistent and unique to that artist's improvisational style.

Licks and Phrases
Sometimes, transcribing an entire solo can be more work than is called for. This is especially true if you're in love with a particular phrase in a solo that you find otherwise uninspiring. It creates a lot of extra work to transcribe more than the phrase in question, unless you choose to tackle the whole thing as an exercise. By focusing on isolated licks that you find inspiring or particularly evocative of a style, you free up time to explore those licks in greater depth. There is no law saying that if you take on fewer than 32 measures, you'll have your transcription license revoked.

Progressions and Substitutions
In many ways, this type of transcription is more relevant to the topics in the book *Jazz Keyboard Harmony* than to this book. However, *substitutions* (alternate sets of chord changes) and other chord progressions are often used as tools to stimulate material for improvisation. Sometimes you will hear a standard played with an intriguing set of changes and your main goal in these cases may simply be to find those chords.

Tunes
Transcription as a means of learning tunes is discussed in greater depth in the "Tunes" section that begins on page 134. In some cases, the process is almost indistinguishable from that of transcribing a solo. For example, many bebop melodies present the same types of language as improvised solos. In these cases, transcribing the melody can be quite similar to transcribing a chorus of an improvised solo, aside from the additional need to figure out the changes.

How to Transcribe: Two Methods

Method 1: Write down every note

Perhaps the most common method of transcription is to write down exactly what you hear. For this method, it's tremendously useful to have a tape or CD player with pitch control. Because recordings are not always perfectly in tune with your keyboard instrument of choice, it's helpful to be able to adjust the pitch on a recording so that you can work on a transcription in the "true" key. Another benefit of certain pitch-controllable machines is the capacity for half-speed playback. This way, the pitch remains the same (although generally lowered by an octave), and you can slow down the music to more easily hear individual elements. Your next option is to use a keyboard with pitch control and to adjust accordingly.

Try out the following step-by-step transcription process. Use the example provided on the CD or a four-measure passage from another recording. Begin with something manageable; even a simple rock or folk tune will work. Each of the answers is shown upside down.

A. Figure out the key. Unless you have perfect pitch, this will probably consist of listening to the example a few times and homing in on the correct key using the keyboard as a reference.

Answer (all answers are upside down):

This passage is in the key of C.

B. Figure out the chord progression. If you're already familiar with a tune, analyzing the chord progression may be easy. Otherwise, you'll want to figure out the changes before trying to transcribe the melodic lines, since the harmony is in most cases is a direct source of melody notes. Try hearing the movement of the roots first, then experiment with the chords, playing along with the recording. Always begin with the most logical chord choices, then move on to other possibilities.

Answer:

C. Figure out the rhythms. Having determined the chord progression, move on to the rhythms. Listen to the whole passage several times. Determine the time signature. Then, take it a little bit at a time and figure out each fragment. Unless you have impeccable ears, this will involve a certain amount of stopping and rewinding, stopping and rewinding.

Answer:

D. Figure out the contour of the melody. Before you get to actual pitches, sketch out a simple contour diagram using the rhythms you've already figured out. Make note of where the melody moves up and down, and whether it does so by step or by leap.

Answer:

E. Figure out the pitches of the melody. Use the chord progression as a basis for educated guesses about note choices. For example, if you hear a note that sounds very *inside* (doesn't clash with the chords), chances are it's a note from the underlying chord, or at least a note from the key.

Answer:

Once you have your transcription on paper, there are a number of things you can do with it. Analyze it, sight-sing it or learn it at the keyboard.

Method 2: Learn with Ear and Memory

In many ways, this method is the same as the previous one, since in both cases you're trying to figure out exactly what was played by the artist you're transcribing. The main difference is that this method takes a somewhat less mechanical approach. Your first step is to be able to sing along with everything, be it a single lick or an entire solo. In the latter case, you'll need a fair amount of practice and a good memory to be able to sing everything. You'll find it worthwhile, however, since learning this way makes you tune in more to phrasing, feel and other intangibles that are completely missing from a written page. Dynamics, range, rhythm and contour will also likely be better internalized when learned in this fashion. To prepare for this method, you may want to listen to such masters of *scat*-style singing (using nonsense syllables to articulate the notes) as Louis Armstrong, Ella Fitzgerald and Jon Hendricks. That way, you'll develop some scatting vocabulary and not be limited to "la-la-la" every time you sing.

What you do with a melodic passage that you've learned to sing in this way depends on your specific goals. In some cases, you're already done if your goal was to tune in with the feel, phrasing and contour of a solo or artist. If you want to use the exact notes at the keyboard, the next step is to apply the sung passage in your head to the keyboard. If you want, you can go back to the recording to check for accuracy. If you wish to analyze the passage further, you now have all the knowledge you need to write it down. As an ear-training exercise, you can also go straight from singing to writing down the tune, and then go back to check your accuracy.

Summary

Each of these transcription methods is useful in its own way, and a well-rounded jazz musician will invariably develop the skills to use each and will find applications for each. You're encouraged to do just that. Even if you find one method more consistently useful than another, don't lose sight of the benefits you can reap from other methods.

Finally, as you sit down to transcribe, go in with a clear idea of what you're trying to accomplish, and choose the method most compatible with your goal. If you find something irresistible about John Patton's swing feel at the organ or Al Haig's touch at the piano, you're unlikely to tap into that by transcribing one of their solos on paper and analyzing it mathematically. On the other hand, if you're intrigued by a specific Roger Kellaway substitution or Dodo Marmarosa's note choices when soloing on a particular ii–V–I progression, notating and analyzing it in that way may be just the ticket. As with all other modes of practicing, you should work to make your methods fit your needs and goals.

APPLYING "HEARD" CONTOURS TO A TUNE

Picture this: You're playing a solo, and a brilliant line comes into your head. It may be original, or it may be something that you heard someone else play. Whatever the source, it has just the sound that your solo needs at that moment. But there's only one problem: It's a line you've never actually played before. So, without asking the band to hold on a minute while you find the recording and transcribe the line, how do you put this material to use in your solo?

Here's where your understanding of rhythm and contour combines with your other musical knowledge to give you exactly what you need in this situation. Let's say the line goes something like this:

The key is to grasp the rhythm and contour of the line. The makeup of the overall contour may be summarized as follows:

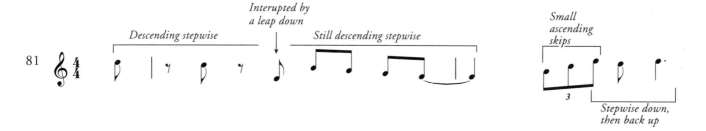

Once you have figured out the contour, you can apply that contour to whatever changes you're dealing with at that moment. All you need to do is pay attention to the restrictions of the harmony. If, for example, it's a stepwise passage, make sure that you use a scale compatible with the key you're in; if it's an arpeggio, be aware of the notes in the underlying chord(s)—though, as always, you can choose whether or not to play those notes.

As an example, let's look at the following eight-measure progression. The changes are in the style of those used on the A section of "There Will Never Be Another You," a popular standard recorded by such saxophonists as Coleman Hawkins, Lester Young, Sonny Rollins, James Moody, Gerry Mulligan, Art Pepper and Dexter Gordon.

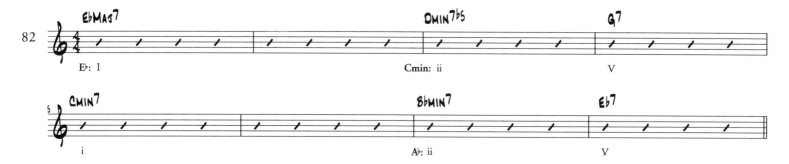

Now, in examples 83–89, try out the melodic pattern from example 80 with different two-bar sections from the changes in example 82.

Measures 1 and 2:

Measures 2 and 3:

Measures 3 and 4:

Measures 4 and 5:

Measures 5 and 6:

Measures 6 and 7:

Measures 7 and 8:

Of course, there even more ways to make this (or any) contour fit over these changes. As with the other concepts you've learned, as you musical vocabulary increases, so do the possibilities.

INTERACTION

All the tools and techniques we've examined so far will help you to decide what to play and how to play it when it comes time to improvise a solo. However, if you ever intend to play for or with others, there is another area that warrants some attention: interaction with others. There are, of course, many ways in which interaction is relevant to playing jazz, but because this book focuses on improvisation, we'll look at some interaction-related topics that will specifically impact the way you improvise.

The Audience. Interaction with an audience can be subtle. Still, there are ways in which an audience can definitely impact your improvisation. As you become more experienced, you'll develop the ability to gauge the energy of the room. If that energy is very subdued or very prominent, you can react accordingly when choosing how to play. Then, there is the matter of audience focus. If the audience is listening intently and enthusiastically, feed off that energy and let it inspire your best and most focused improvisation. If the audience is indifferent, don't take it personally or allow it to throw off your focus.

The Drums. The drums have multiple roles in a jazz setting. One is to keep time and lay down a good *pocket* (exact placement of the beat), creating a *groove* (the musical flow that results when all players are in rhythmic sync). Another is to play stimulating rhythms on top of that pocket. As a keyboard soloist in a band with drums, you must first make sure that your phrasing is rhythmically compatible with the drummer's pocket. As for the drummer's other rhythms, consider them "there for the taking"—that is, do anything you want with them except ignore them. Play similar rhythms, or use contrasting ones; respond to busy drumming by playing busily yourself, or by playing sparsely and letting the drummer handle the busy stuff. It's up to you. The drums also have a direct and substantial impact on the overall volume level, so you and the drummer should interact accordingly. Ideally, this will occur in a manner so natural and instinctive that neither of you can tell who initiates the dynamic changes. In some cases, however, you'll simply need to either lead or follow dynamically. Another aspect of interaction with the drums is *trading*, in which the melodic soloists trade off solo fragments—usually, four bars (called *trading fours*) or eight bars—with the drummer.

The Bass. The bass is typically positioned between the drums and the keyboard, and for good reason. The bassist in a jazz group shares responsibility for the pocket with the drummer and for the harmonies with the keyboard or other harmony instrument(s). The way you lock in with and interact with the bassist reflects this dual role. As with the drummer, you must hook up with the bassist's pocket (which is hopefully in sync with the drummer's pocket). You should also pay attention to ensure that your harmonies are compatible with what the bass is playing. It's possible, especially if you're playing organ, that you're handling bass duties at the same time that you're improvising. In this case, make doubly sure that you're in sync with the drums, and don't allow the bass element (that is, your feet or left hand) to make your playing too predictable.

The Chords. Obviously, your note choices in a solo must take the chords into consideration. The rhythms used for the chords can also have an impact on the rhythms you choose in your solo. If you're playing with a guitarist or vibraphonist, all of this is another example of listening to and locking in with another player. If you're the player responsible for the chords, your right hand (the "soloist") interacts with the chords in your left hand. In the keyboard music you've learned, you've probably already used your hands in different, independent roles.

Comping (chordal accompaniment) is mostly beyond the scope of this book, but let's take a quick look at some of the choices you can make in the interaction of your left and right hands. You can choose, for example, to play left-hand chords in a way that accentuates and matches up with the accented notes in the right hand.

You can also take the opposite approach, using the left hand to fill in the gaps during rests or rhythmically static parts in the right hand.

Another choice you can make is how full you want your voicings to be. If, for example, you have a very simple melodic line, you can choose sparse voicings to accentuate the simplicity. You could also choose to use richer chord voicings in that situation, using the left hand to pick up the slack for the minimal activity in the right hand.

The same choice exists if the melody is more active. Sparser chords can help to avoid getting in the way of a melody line with more notes, while richer chords will add to the drama. The more you learn about different types of chord voicings, the more significant these choices become.

As with most of the choices you must make as a player, there are no rights or wrongs when it comes to chords—just different options, each with its own impact. The key is to be aware of your options and the impact of each one. Work towards being able to use your left hand to enhance your solos.

PUTTING IT TOGETHER

On the next few pages, we'll look at some examples that combine the elements we've seen in this chapter. Example 94, which continues on page 47, represent a one-chorus solo over an AABA form. The changes are in the style of those in Jerome Kern's "The Way You Look Tonight," a tune recorded by the likes of Art Tatum, Wes Montgomery, Stephane Grappelli, Teddy Wilson and Johnny Griffin. The first A section uses the major scale, the second A uses chord tones, the bridge (B) uses the major pentatonic scale, and the last A, which has a four-bar tag, uses a combination of all three. The other elements you've learned about in this chapter (syncopation, patterns, etc.) are incorporated throughout. Your left hand can comp using voicings with which you're comfortable.

The sample solo in example 95 uses the same elements as those in example 94. Because the tune passes repeatedly through minor keys, you'll also find the scales we looked at in "Minor Scale Options" on page 29. The changes are in the style of those used by George Shearing in the modern jazz standard "Lullaby of Birdland," a tune has been recorded by a who's who of jazz pianists, including Shearing, Earl Hines, Teddy Wilson, Duke Ellington, Count Basie, Ahmad Jamal, Erroll Garner, Bud Powell, Billy Taylor, Jimmy Rowles and Jaki Byard.

Beginning on page 78, we'll examine the blues, including the numerous variations on the 12-bar blues form. Now, we'll take an introductory look, since the 12-bar blues is used in so much of the jazz repertoire. As for phrasing, rhythm, contour and so on, the approach to improvising over a 12-bar blues is the same as that for any other swing-feel jazz tune. Indeed, the flavor of the blues is a large part of what makes up a jazz feel. Here are some guidelines for note choices to use with 12-bar blues, based on the materials we've looked at so far. Note that major and minor scales are usually not applicable in this context, since a true blues conforms to neither a major nor a minor key.

Chord Tones: Chord tones sound good, and they're always a safe bet if you're unsure about scales.

Blues Scale: The gritty sound of the blues scale is wholly appropriate to a blues progression. The ♭3, ♭5 and ♭7 may at times clash with chord tones, but the tension these "blue" notes create is part of the distinctive blues sound. When the use of the blues scale is combined with rhythmic variety and a convincing feel, the perception of dissonance is lessened even further.

Major Pentatonic: This scale sounds great over a blues—except for the IV chord—so be sure to use it accordingly. Unlike the blue notes in the blues scale, the major 3 (in B♭, the note is D) of the major pentatonic scale is a "happy" note that clashes unpleasantly with the ♭7 (in B♭, the note is D♭) of the IV chord.

Example 96 demonstrates these possibilities in two choruses of a typical jazz-style blues in the key of B♭. The first chorus goes from the blues scale (measures 1–4) to chord tones (measures 5–8) to the major pentatonic scale (measures 9–12). The second chorus (measures 13–24) combines all of these elements.

CONCEPTUAL CORNER:
DIFFERENT KEYBOARDS

Most of the tips and techniques we've used so far, as well as those we'll explore in future chapters, apply to improvisation not only on the piano, but also on any other keyboard instrument. Still, every keyboard instrument has qualities and capabilities that are distinctly different from those of the piano. In this Conceptual Corner, we'll compare and contrast the different keyboard instruments, the advantages and disadvantages of each, and how each might impact the way you play.

Piano

Love it or hate it—most of us love it when it's good and hate it when it's bad—the acoustic piano is the undisputed almighty ruler of the jazz keyboard world. Until organ genius Jimmy Smith came around in the 1950s, the instrument faced little competition; even today, however, the majority of straight-ahead jazz still makes use of the good old piano. The sensitivity of touch, tone and dynamic that you get from a fine piano is positively unmatched by any other keyboard instrument. If you can perform on a first-rate piano, relish the opportunity. If you can own one, it is a joy and can even be a wise financial investment; unlike a car, a high-level piano will often retain its value if well maintained.

While the pros of the piano as a performing instrument are significant, pianos are not without cons. From a consumer's standpoint, they're expensive. They're not easily portable; you can't take one to a gig or fold it up and put it in the closet when you need more space. They require regular maintenance; a piano should be tuned twice a year for normal use, more often if used for performing. If the piano is kept in a space in which temperature and humidity conditions aren't optimal, it may barely hold its tune at all.

The most significant drawback of a piano presents itself when you're forced to play on someone else's inadequate piano, especially in a performance situation. So, what do you do in a situation like this? There are several ways you can deal with a subpar piano. One is to grin and bear it, play your usual stuff and absolve yourself of any responsibility for unpleasant sounds that aren't your fault. Or, you can avoid having to tackle the instrument entirely, provided you can bring a portable keyboard of your own.

If neither of these options works for you, there are still some things you can do to help the situation. If the piano is out of tune, try to adjust accordingly. Even on such an instrument, sparse, dissonant or high-energy sounds all have some chance of working, while lush, colorful sonorities are more likely to emphasize the out-of-tuneness. For some perspective on this issue, check out live recordings like Eric Dolphy's *At the Five Spot* series (with Mal Waldron on piano) and John Coltrane's *Live at Birdland* (with McCoy Tyner on piano). In both cases, the pianists do an admirable job of dealing with less-than-ideal pianos.

Another problem that sometimes arises with pianos is an instrument that is too soft. If, for example, you're playing in a quintet, but the piano is a delicate spinet-style instrument with no additional amplification, you're likely to encounter projection problems. In an ideal world, the solution would be as simple as having the other band members play more softly to compensate, but that isn't always possible. When it comes time to solo in that situation, don't hurt yourself. The natural tendency is to bash the keys harder to project, but you must remember that bashing won't make a spinet into a concert grand. If you're sensing that your solo lines aren't projecting well, try using block chords or octaves (see pages 60, 94–95 and 120–121), both of which will help you cut through a band. In fact, the octave style popularized by Phineas Newborn, Jr. is said to have been developed in part to deal with projection problems.

Organ

A number of pre-bop keyboardists, including Wild Bill Davis and Fats Waller, made use of the organ, but it was not then a mainstream jazz instrument. Since Jimmy Smith's rise to prominence, the Hammond B-3 organ has been a fairly popular jazz keyboard option. In the 1960s, especially, players like Smith, Brother Jack McDuff, Jimmy McGriff and Shirley Scott made it the keyboard instrument of choice for blues-drenched soul jazz. As the decade progressed, Larry Young incorporated modern devices à la McCoy Tyner, and Don Patterson used more of the bebop language than most other organ players. In the 1990s, young lions like Joey DeFrancesco, John Medeski and Larry Goldings (all of them also pianists) began to use the organ in more eclectic ways.

Still, the soul jazz connection to the organ is strong, and it exists for a reason. The organist is very often responsible for using the feet and/or left hand to provide a bass line. While a great organist can play a skillful solo while also providing a bass line, the responsibility of playing a bass line naturally leads to a tendency to play simpler phrases in the right hand. There is also something about the tone of the organ that lends itself to soul jazz. The sustain and volume that can be achieved by a single note on the organ, so conducive to a wailing blues sound, far outweigh the same qualities on the piano. On the other hand, the melodic range that is useful for an organ solo is fairly limited, attacks are often less clear than those on a piano, and control of dynamics applies uniformly throughout the instrument and is restricted to the use of a volume pedal as opposed to the key-by-key, note-by-note nuances possible on a piano. All of these factors make intricate bebop phrasing more difficult, though not impossible, on the organ.

In addition, real fluency on the organ entails fluency with all those darned knobs and bars. It's possible to play a perfectly decent organ solo with a "piano" conception, but the instrument has unique elements and characteristics that require study and experimentation on the part of players who want to fully exploit the organ's possibilities. First and foremost are the *drawbars* or *drawstops*. If you check out a pipe organ in a church or concert hall, you'll see an array of knobs by the keyboard whose function is to control which set of pipes is sounding at any given moment. No pipes means no sound, while all of them means the most over-the-top sound possible (hence the phrase "pulling out all the stops"). The B-3 and similar instruments, since they don't use actual pipes, simulate "stop" effects electronically, controlled by the drawbars. Therefore, a familiarity with the drawbars and the varied possibilities they provide is important. A skilled organist will likely make drawbar adjustments for different sorts of tunes, or even for different effects within a single tune.

The percussion settings on many organs are another commonly used tool. Using these adds a *harmonic* (overtone) that creates a percussive effect at the moment the note is struck. This effect is often used for solos, as it makes the articulation clearer. Organists also often use settings that add *vibrato* (a very rapid and slight pitch fluctuation) or chorus effects for a richer, more complex sound. Of course, the famous Leslie speaker, a vital element of the B-3 sound, is an effect in itself. You can adjust the speed of the rotation (which produces the Leslie's distinctive waver) from slow to fast, producing different results. Keep in mind that a fast rotation speed is generally less compatible with subtle or clearly articulated single-note passages, while it can be very effective with dramatic sustained notes, tremolos, and so on. Finally, there is the volume pedal. Some people use it to constantly shape the volume of their playing; others use it only when they need to subtly raise or lower the overall volume. In either case, remember that the volume pedal impacts the overall effect, but it doesn't offer the subtle gradations in dynamic that are possible on a piano.

Once upon a time, many jazz venues had their own B-3, but that is no longer true. A devoted shopper can still find an original B-3 with a rotating Leslie speaker, the magical combination that defines the jazz organ sound. While it is possible to take a B-3 apart to transport it to and from a gig, it isn't easy, and it requires at least a van—and, even better, a road crew. Most organists nowadays use electronic keyboards that are easier to maintain and much more portable. Several MIDI organ units have Hammond-style drawbars and provide a remarkable recreation of the B-3 sound. Some come with a simulated Leslie effect, though many organists simply run the portable organ through a real Leslie speaker. If you're not using a Leslie, make sure your keyboard amp can handle the volume and range of the organ.

Electric Piano

By the end of the 1960s, electric (not to be confused with electronic; see below) pianos had become popular with some jazz players, and that popularity remained high throughout the 1970s. The (Fender) Rhodes was by far the most common electric piano in jazz, with the Wurlitzer ranking second. While the sound of the Rhodes was largely identified with funk and other crossover styles, it's also far from incompatible with straight-ahead jazz. In the 1970s, in fact, pianists from Kenny Barron and Cedar Walton to Bill Evans and Oscar Peterson—all players associated primarily with the acoustic piano— made creative use of the Rhodes in a straight-ahead setting. By the 1980s, electric pianos fell out of fashion, but since then the Rhodes has made a bit of a comeback. Younger pianists like David Berkman, George Colligan and Uri Caine have helped spur the resurgence of the Rhodes in a modern jazz setting.

What an electric piano has going for it above all is that it's essentially an acoustic instrument with amplification. Just like an electric guitar, it makes a sound whether it's plugged in or not, and pickups are used to amplify that sound. The touch, dynamics and acoustics of an electric piano therefore provide the closest approximation to the real thing. The sound of the instrument itself is entirely a matter of personal taste (and perhaps that of the people who hire you); some people adore it, while others find it tacky. Another benefit of electric pianos is the price; a used Rhodes in good condition that you find in a classified ad will invariably be cheaper than even a bottom-of-the-line digital piano (see below). For those who insist on the "organic" feeling of an acoustic instrument, electric pianos are often more practical than acoustic ones. For example, people in apartments and/or people who move with some frequency will appreciate the relative portability of an electric piano. And, unlike a piano, you can turn the volume down or turn the amplifier off, a benefit if you have neighbors or roommates. Assuming you like the sound, the downsides to electric pianos are weight and repairs. While an electric piano is portable, it isn't light, so transporting it to gigs is not always easy. And, because the instruments are relics of decades past, repairing your Rhodes can be much like fixing an old car—as time passes, fewer and fewer people will know how to fix it, stock the correct parts, and so on.

Digital Piano

Unlike an electric piano, a digital piano is an entirely electronic machine. There is no sound unless you turn on the electricity, the sounds come from digital samples, and the dynamics come from numerical messages triggered by the velocity with which you hit the key. Any highly skilled pianist can instantly tell the difference between the touch, sound and responsiveness of a digital piano versus a "real" one. The reasons for using a digital piano over a good acoustic piano are almost entirely logistical, as opposed to musical. That said, logistics are often hard to deny, and digital pianos are much like more common types of computers—as the technology gets better and cheaper, fewer people do their day-to-day business without them. With each passing year, digital pianos are manufactured with better sound and touch. Many more people are buying them for their homes, as they can be moved around more easily than acoustic pianos and never need to be tuned. For working jazz pianists who need to bring their own equipment, digital pianos have become the most common solution. And while a digital piano can't compare with a gorgeous Steinway concert grand, it sure beats the barely playable spinets at some venues.

When shopping for a digital piano, there are many features to evaluate, so you should go into the process with a clear picture of your needs and budget. There are a lot of bells and whistles that you can get, like sequencers, huge banks of different sounds, etc. If those are appealing and/or important, then expect to pay a premium for them. If all you want is the effect of having a piano, shop for a model with fewer frills. One option is to buy a keyboard with few or no sounds (a keyboard with no on-board sounds is called a *MIDI controller*), as long as you like the touch. Then, via MIDI, you can buy and use a sampler or sound module to produce the piano sound you want. Make sure you buy a keyboard with touch sensitivity, weighted keys, MIDI compatibility and a feel you like. Make sure you have enough keys. For some people, 88 keys are necessary, for others, 72 will suffice and five octaves are the absolute minimum.

Synthesizer

To synthesize is to combine parts into a whole, and in music, a synthesizer is an electronic instrument that combines various sounds into a single instrument. In practical terms, a synthesizer is nowadays defined as an electronic keyboard of whatever sort. In the very early days of synthesizers, they were huge machines (sometimes taking up the better part of a room) and didn't necessarily have keyboards attached to them. By the late 1960s, portable (or at least semi-portable) analog synthesizers like the Moog and the ARP were being used by keyboardists like Chick Corea, Herbie Hancock and Joe Zawinul—all innovators in what would later be referred to as "fusion." These were monophonic synthesizers, meaning you could only play one note at a time on them. Soon polyphonic synthesizers were being made. When digital synthesizers became common in the 1980s (notably the Yamaha DX7), they quickly became popular, as they were more portable and easier to use, and had a greater ability to imitate "real" instruments. That popularity continues to this day, though some people still use analog synths for a "vintage" sound. Much of synthesizer development also revolved around MIDI (musical instrument digital interface) whereby synths and other digital music machines can be linked together. So, as described in the section on digital pianos, it is possible to have a keyboard that gets all of its sounds from another source. You play a note on the keyboard, which triggers the appropriate sound from the module or sampler, as communicated through a MIDI cable. Or, you can use the keyboard to enter data into a sequencer (the MIDI equivalent of a multi-track recording machine) that is either in the keyboard itself, in a separate unit, or existing as a piece of software on a computer.

Hopefully, you are getting the idea that there are many different types of synthesizers and many different uses for them. You can buy a synthesizer at a department store for $50 or you can buy one from a musical instrument dealer for $5000. Some synthesizers and synth features are directly relevant to a jazz player, some are more peripherally relevant, and some are not terribly relevant at all. We have already discussed types of synthesizers that simulate the effect of a piano or Hammond B-3 organ, trying to replicate the sound and touch of the "real" instruments. In a straight-ahead jazz context, these are the most directly relevant uses of synthesizers. There is some debate as to the usefulness of synthesizers that sound like synthesizers (as opposed to trying to sound like identifiable acoustic instruments). While synthesizers are essential to fusion, jazz-pop and other such styles, they never quite caught on in straight-ahead jazz, in spite of a brief period in which excited jazz pianists trotted out their DX7s for gigs or recordings. The capacity for using a variety of sounds, for being able to alter those sounds and for embellishing notes with the "pitch bend" and "modulation" controls, all have great expressive possibilities, though again, the resulting sounds primarily have been used outside of the context of straight-ahead jazz. Thus the advice regarding the use of synthesizers in this way is much like the advice about electric pianos. It is up to personal choice (yours and that of your musical employers) whether you want to make use of that world of sounds in your playing.

There are some very practical functions of synthesizers that can be relevant to a jazz player. In the section on digital pianos, you were advised to make sure that you have enough keys and that the keys are weighted. That advice still stands for situations where you are going for the utmost in piano-like effect, but what about situations where that is unnecessary or even excessive? For example, a synthesizer can be very useful for transcribing (especially because of the capacity for pitch control). It can be useful for using a sequencer, so that you can work out and hear ideas that use multiple voices, or hear an up-tempo version of something that you can't play that fast yet yourself. It can be useful for data entry if you choose to do your music notation (tunes, transcriptions or whatever else) on the computer rather than by hand. In all of these cases, a digital piano is not a bad choice, but it is likely overkill. In some cases, a digital piano's size and weight (you can't have weighted keys without packing on some poundage) is simply impractical, especially in certain travelling situations. Let's say, for example, that you have a gig for which you have to carry all your gear for ten blocks from the bus stop. If you're using a non-weighted synthesizer in a piano-like setting for this sort of reason, make sure it is at least velocity sensitive. And, when you play it, keep the limitations in mind, so that you don't hurt yourself trying to coax out sounds that aren't there.

CHAPTER 3

MODES OF THE MAJOR SCALE

If a scale is a series of single notes that progresses stepwise up or down, a *mode* of that scale contains the same notes, but starts and ends in a different place. We already explored this phenomenon when looking at relative major and minor scales. The natural minor is actually the 6th mode of the major scale. Each mode has a name carried over from ancient Greece.

MODE	NAME
1st	Ionian
2nd	Dorian
3rd	Phrygian
4th	Lydian
5th	Mixolydian
6th	Aeolian
7th	Locrian

One way to learn the modes of the major scale is to relate everything to the *parent scale*, the scale from which you are deriving the other modes. As such, you should practice all seven modes (one for each note in the scale) of each of the 12 major scales. Example 97 shows the modes of the C Major scale.

1st Mode: C Ionian (same as major)

97

2nd Mode: D Dorian   3rd Mode: E Phrygian

4th Mode: F Lydian   5th Mode: G Mixolydian

6th Mode: A Aeolian (same as natural minor)   7th Mode: B Locrian

MODES AS AUTONOMOUS SCALES

The word "mode" can also be a synonym for the word "scale." In other words, modes can be thought of as scales, each with its own identity separate from that of the parent scale. One effect of this (which we will soon explore further) is that each mode relates to a particular chord.

Learning modes in this way is just as important as learning them in relation to the parent scale, and any well-rounded jazz musician can do both in all 12 keys.

MODE	NUMERIC FORMULA	CHORD IMPLIED
Ionian	1, 2, 3, 4, 5, 6, 7, 1	Maj7 (or 6)
Dorian	1, 2, ♭3, 4, 5, 6, ♭7, 1	min7 (or min6)
Phrygian	1, ♭2, ♭3, 4, 5, ♭6, ♭7, 1	min7
Lydian	1, 2, 3, ♯4, 5, 6, 7, 1	Maj7
Mixolydian	1, 2, 3, 4, 5, 6, ♭7, 1	Dominant 7
Aeolian	1, 2, ♭3, 4, 5, ♭6, ♭7, 1	min7
Locrian	1, ♭2, ♭3, 4, ♭5, ♭6, ♭7, 1	min7♭5

Here are the seven modes, each starting on C. Practice each mode in all 12 keys, one mode at a time.

1st Mode: C Ionian

98

2nd Mode: C Dorian   3rd Mode: C Phrygian

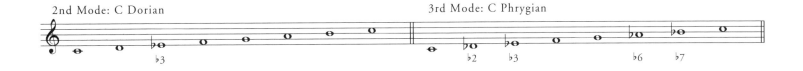

4th Mode: C Lydian   5th Mode: C Mixolydian

6th Mode: C Aeolian   7th Mode: C Locrian

Non-Chord Tones

Non-chord tones are nothing new—any time you play a scale, you are invariably playing some non-chord tones. Likewise, there are times when you'll add notes that are not typically thought of as part of the chord. On page 58, we will learn about extensions, a variation on this phenomenon. However, there are also times when non-chord tones are chosen specifically because they provide contrast with chord tones. Using a C Major triad to designate chord tones, here are some ways in which musicians employ non-chord tones. For clarity, the chord tones are shown as whole notes.

A *passing tone* is a note that comes between two "main" notes. The sound of the main notes is so emphatic that any tension caused by the passing tone is quickly resolved.

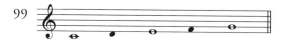

An *approach tone* is a note that falls next to (directly above or below) the main note and is played before that main note. Landing on the main note resolves the tension created by the non-chord tone.

A *neighbor tone* is like an approach tone in that it is found next to the main note. A neighbor tone, however, is played after the main note, usually returning to the main note.

Ornaments

An *ornament* is something used for decoration. A tasteful ornament spruces up the main object (hood of a car, Christmas tree), but does not detract attention from it. Such is the case in music. A musical ornament emphasizes or decorates a note through the use of other notes.

Here are some common ornaments that are a bit more specific than simply utilizing the non-chord tones shown above. You'll pick up the rest through listening to a lot of jazz, where ornamentation is often improvised. For the examples below, the smaller notes denote ornaments and the larger notes denote the main notes, still outlining a C Major triad.

The *grace note* is one of the most widely used ornaments in jazz. To play a grace note, you move very quickly from an upper or lower approach tone to the main note, creating a sort of "crushed note" effect.

While a grace note is a single note, a *turn* is a series of notes. Specifically, you begin with the main note, step to a neighbor tone, return to the main note, step to the neighbor tone in the other direction, and return to the main note. Usually, turns are played quickly and without rhythmic emphasis.

The *enclosure* is much like the turn in the way it surrounds the main note. However, to play an enclosure, you play the two neighbor tones, then you land on the main note. An enclosure can be played quickly or with a more "normal" rhythm.

CHROMATIC NOTES

The *chromatic scale* is the 12-note scale that contains every different pitch on the keyboard (or, for that matter, in the language of Western music). Taken as a scale, it is just a series of half steps—and, good news, there's only one chromatic scale, so there's no need to play it in all 12 keys.

Chromatic Ornaments

The same ornaments we examined starting on page 56 can be used with notes from the chromatic scale. While the ornamental notes we used were diatonic, we can also use the chromatic versions of each of these—simply play the note a half step away from the main note. In some cases there is overlap, as the nearest note may actually be a diatonic note (a note in the key you're in). The examples below will show you some of the ways that you can apply chromaticism to non-chord tones and ornamentation.

Chromatic Passing Tones (shown with C Major scale)   Chromatic Approach Tones   Chromatic Neighbor Tones

Chromatic Grace Notes   Chromatic Turns   Chromatic Enclosures

Bebop Scale

The *bebop scale* actually refers to two different scales. One, the *dominant bebop scale*, is similar to the Mixolydian mode and is used with dominant 7th chords. The other, the *minor bebop scale*, is similar to the Dorian mode and is used with minor 7th chords. In each case, the bebop scale can be derived by taking the other scales mentioned (Mixolydian and Dorian) and adding a chromatic passing tone in the space between ♭7 and 1. Example 107 shows both of these scales in C.

C Dominant Bebop Scale   C Minor Bebop Scale

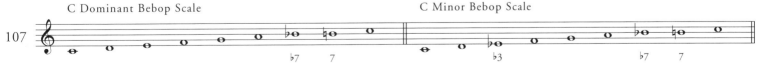

CHORD EXTENSIONS

By turning triads into 7th chords, we've already looked at ways of adding notes to a chord to achieve a richer sound. Modern jazz pianists often add *extensions* (often called *color tones* or just *colors*) to chords for still more richness. These tones can also be incorporated into one's improvisation.

Take a look at the C Major 7th chord to the right. It is a series of stacked 3rds, or a scale (in this case, C Lydian) in which every other note is skipped. If you continue stacking 3rds, you wind up with 9, #11 and 13. In a scale, you would call these notes 2, #4 and 6, but the numbers 9, 11 and 13 are used instead to clarify that these notes are in the second oc-tave. From a structural standpoint, they're not among the fundamental chord tones, but rather added on top of them. Notice how the #11 avoids clashing with the 3rd in the chord in a way that a ♮11 would be unable to do. Example 109 shows the extensions most commonly used on 7th and 6th chords.

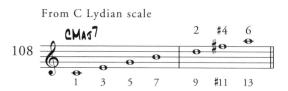

From C Lydian scale

Notice the gray notes in several of the chords in example 109 (7, min6 and dim7). These are notes that can be used with these chords, but which slightly change the chord's identity rather than functioning as an extension.

Because a ♮11 on a dominant 7th chord clashes so much with the 3rd, that note should be used instead of the 3rd. This creates a "suspended" chord, in which case the 11 is called 4. The major 7th can be used with both minor 6th and diminished 7th chords, but it likewise tends to take the place of the 6th (♭♭7) in either chord rather than serving as an extension. These differences are shown in example 110.

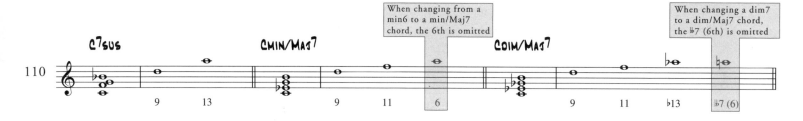

Altered Dominant Chords

All of the chord extensions above are meant to add color to a chord without fundamentally altering its identity. However, there is one case in which altering a chord's identity is frequently useful. *Resolving dominant chords* are dominant 7th chords that in one way or another serve the function of resolving to other chords. Because these chords resolve (not always the case with dominant 7th chords), they can handle colors that introduce more tension to their sounds. The four tones in example 111 are used in various combinations with the root, 3rd and 7th of a dominant chord to create an *altered dominant* or just *altered chord,* which adds extra tension to the chord.

SUBSTITUTION

While substitution is primarily a harmonic technique, it also applies to soloing, so we'll take a brief look at it here. (See Chapter 5 of *Jazz Keyboard Harmony* for a more thorough explanation of chord substitution.)

When you see a set of changes in a tune, you're not always required or even expected to follow it verbatim. In a jazz context, *substitution* is the act of taking an existing chord progression and adding or changing chords. Substitution can be prearranged, or it can happen spontaneously. The fundamental principle is that significant points of tonal resolution should be left alone. The function of substitution is to provide varied and stimulating journeys to these established points of resolution, so the approach is to find a point of resolution and then work backwards. Let's look at some common substitution techniques, beginning with the four-bar progression in example 112. The fifth bar, CMaj7, is included here as a point of resolution towards which the substitutions will lead.

One common and basic substitution practice is to expand a V chord into a ii–V, as in example 113A. In turn, you can expand the expansion by approaching it through root movement in 5ths, as in example 11B.

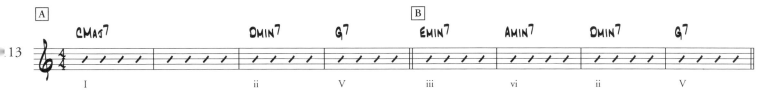

Dominant cycles create a sort of domino effect, whereby a dominant chord "resolves" to another dominant chord, as in example 114A. Such cycles can be stretched out to include several chords, as in example 114B.

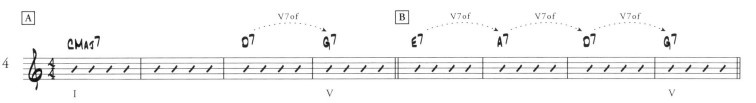

In *tritone substitution,* you can add color by replacing a dominant 7th chord with the dominant 7th chord a tritone away, as in example 115A. You can create even more tension and surprise by preceding this new chord with the chord a 5th above, as in example 115B.

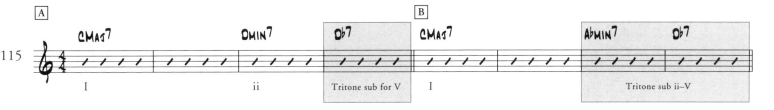

One reason the tritone substitution works is that the 3rd and ♭7 of the substitution chord are the ♭7 and 3rd (respectively) of the dominant chord. Usually, one or both of these will be enharmonically respelled in the substitution chord.

BLUES DEVICES

Some devices and ornaments are strongly associated with the sound of the blues. Some that we have already looked at, like grace notes, can be very evocative of the blues, but can also be used for other purposes; others are virtually inseparable from the blues sound. This section will lay out and provide examples of some devices that are associated with blues keyboard and which a jazz player can use to impart a blues feeling while improvising. Play all of these examples at a medium-slow tempo.

To play a *tremolo*, alternate between two notes as quickly as possible for a fluttering effect.

Crushed notes, which involve playing a series of notes very quickly without bringing out the articulation of individual notes, create a sweeping or smearing effect.

A *double-stop* is a pair of notes played simultaneously. 3rds and 6ths are common in blues-style playing.

Another popular double-stop technique is to keep the same top note throughout a phrase while the bottom voice moves to create the main melody. Notice how the fingerings in several cases involve sliding the same finger down from a black key to the adjacent white key.

Playing parallel octaves in the right hand is a widely used and dramatic technique. The left-hand chords use the same rhythm as that of the right-hand melody, creating a *block chord* (all notes sounding together) effect.

SHELL VOICINGS AND GUIDE-TONE LINES

Shell Voicings

One of the most widely used types of voicings in all of jazz harmony is the *shell voicing*. As the name indicates, shell voicings are stark and skeletal. The 5th is omitted; the root can be played in the bass register by the left hand or can be omitted entirely and left to the bassist (or whoever is covering the bass tones), leaving the 3rd and 7th of the chord. In addition to being used as they are, shell voicings can also serve as the basis for many more colorful voicings. Shell voicings provide the skeleton around which the chord is fleshed out, since the 3rd and 7th are central to defining the sound of a chord. Example 121 is a iii–vi–ii–V–I progression in shell voicings. If you want to reinforce the sound, you can play the roots in your left hand.

Notice the consistent smoothness of the voice leading. In this progression, as with most progressions in which the chord roots descend diatonically in 5ths, only one note changes with each successive change of chord. The 7th of each chord steps downward to the 3rd of the following chord while the 3rd of each chord stays put and becomes the 7th of the following chord.

Guide-Tone Lines

Guide-tone lines are melodic lines that emphasize the movement from one of the fundamental tones (3rd or 7th) to another at the moment the chords change. Example 122 shows a simple guide-tone line that continually moves from the 7th of one chord to the 3rd of the next.

While the example above is rhythmically basic, guide-tone lines can also be more involved. The key is that the guide-tone transition occurs as the chords change. The notes can be short or long, anticipated or on the beat, exposed or preceded by other notes. In example 123, the guide tones are highlighted in gray.

𝅗𝅥 = Guide Tone

Note that when dominant cycles are used, the options for guide tones increase—in fact, they usually double. While only one note changes in most cases where chords descend diatonically in 5ths, both notes change when dominant 7th chords descend in 5ths. This is the case also when dominant 7th chords are used in tandem with tritone substitution. Dominant chords a tritone apart share the same guide tones (see page 59, bottom), so the same rules apply.

CONCEPTUAL CORNER:
TENSION AND RELEASE

Picture this: Three versions of a movie are being pitched to a major film executive by three different screenwriters. See if you can guess which one will most likely be chosen.

The starring cast for all three: Good Guy, Good Guy's Gal Pal, Bad Guy.

Version 1: Good Guy is sitting in a field sipping herbal tea with Good Guy's Gal Pal. Good Guy's Gal Pal is suddenly kidnapped by Bad Guy. Good Guy goes on hair-raising quest to rescue Good Guy's Gal Pal. At various times, he comes close to rescuing her, but falls just short. At other moments, he comes close to meeting a perilous end, but narrowly escapes. Then, in a dramatic moment, he rescues Good Guy's Gal Pal. They embrace, breathe a sigh of relief and ride off into the sunset, as Bad Guy utters, "Curses, foiled again!" THE END.

Version 2: Good Guy is sitting in a field sipping herbal tea with Good Guy's Gal Pal. Good Guy's Gal Pal is suddenly kidnapped by Bad Guy. Good Guy stubs his toe while trying to answer his cell phone. The veterinarian calls on the other line to tell Good Guy that his dog is quite ill. He runs to his car, and finds that it won't start. Then, Good Guy gets kidnapped, too. THE END.

Version 3: Good Guy is sitting in a field sipping herbal tea with Good Guy's Gal Pal. They drink some more tea. They take a nap. Upon awakening, they yawn and stretch, and then do some yoga for a while. After yoga, they leisurely sip some more tea and talk calmly about how pleasant the weather is. A refreshing breeze blows. THE END.

If you picked Version 1, you're very perceptive. It follows the always-effective pattern of setting a scene, building tension, and then releasing it, usually with several more small-scale moments of tension and release along the way. Version 2 is all tension and no release, and is likely to be quite unpleasant to most people. Version 3 is all release and no tension and is likely to be quite boring to most people. The dynamic of tension and release is central to what makes compelling theater, cinema, literature—and music. The exact manifestation of the tension and release varies by style, by each individual artist's vision and by personal taste. Some people like very little tension in their music, and others like a tremendous amount. Even people at the extremes of this continuum, however, depend on some degree of tension and release.

If you think you enjoy music with no tension, try playing this example, repeating indefinitely.

If you think you enjoy music with no release, try playing this example, repeating indefinitely.

Very few people will have much tolerance for either of the above examples, and those people are unlikely to have much use for or interest in the information in this book. For the rest of us, the goal is to gain a mastery of the various tools that enable a musician to incorporate tension and release into a compelling improvised solo, and many of the lessons in this book are designed to help develop these tools. Beyond that, it's up to you how much tension you want to build and when and how you want to release it. In any case, you're encouraged to be conscious of the universal effectiveness of tension and release and of how you can harness it.

CHAPTER 4 APPLICATION OF PROFESSIONAL TOOLS

MODAL TUNES

Modal tunes are often defined as tunes whose harmonies are based on modes, in contrast to tunes based on standard diatonic progressions (for example, ii–V–I). One special characteristic of modal tunes is that the *harmonic rhythm* (the rate of change from one chord to the next) tends to be very slow. For example, a single chord may provide the harmony for several measures in a row, reducing the need to negotiate chord changes and allowing you to stick with one mode. Some of the most popular modal tunes include "So What" by Miles Davis, "Maiden Voyage" by Herbie Hancock, "Freedom Jazz Dance" by Eddie Harris and "Little Sunflower" by Freddie Hubbard. The latter tune uses similar changes to those in example 126 (although the form in Hubbard's tune repeats the Dorian section again at the end, creating an AABBAA form). We'll take a more extensive look at playing modal tunes in Chapter 6, but in the meantime, you can use the modes you have practiced to get started playing modal tunes like those listed above. Play this example with a Latin feel, using straight eighth notes.

MAKING THE CHANGES

Making the changes is a jazz term for playing lines that do a good job of delineating the harmonic motion of a chord progression. Many of the most admired soloists in jazz history, from Coleman Hawkins to Sonny Rollins, attained their stature in part through their ability to make the changes within the style of their day. While nobody makes the changes at every moment of every solo (and it would get mighty boring if they did), it's certainly true that being able to make the changes effectively and convincingly is an essential skill for anyone aspiring to improvise in any sort of bebop-inspired setting.

A good test for judging if a line is making the changes is this: If the chord progression is readily apparent from hearing a line alone, the player is probably making the changes. If you can't hear a chord progression except from the rhythm section, then the line is probably not making the changes. Making the changes is simultaneously a subtle art and a straightforward one. There are no hard-and-fast rules that will allow you to clearly distinguish a line that makes the changes from one that does not, but a jazz-trained ear can consistently tell when the changes are or aren't being made.

Play the melody in example 127, which uses notes from the C Major scale over iii–vi–ii–V–I in C.

Now play example 128, which is based on the same scale and rhythms as example 127.

If you have some experience with jazz, chances are that you'll think something sounds a little funny with example 127, while example 128 seems to make more sense. How can that be? After all, we established way back in Chapter 2 that scales within the key of a progression tend to work well as the basis for improvised melodies. Indeed, you can still use scales (and note that example 127 would sound a lot more strange if it were based on a less appropriate scale, such as E♭ Major or F Blues). However, if your goal is to make the changes, chord tones must receive more emphasis than the other notes. By the same token, certain notes in a scale, especially those that don't function as extensions or color tones in a given chord, must be de-emphasized in order to create the impression of making the changes.

Keeping that in mind, play example 129, which uses the same music as in examples 127 and 128 and notice the notes that get the most emphasis (highlighted) in each measure. Notice how the emphasized notes in measures 1–5 relate (or don't relate) to the corresponding chords (they are non-chord tones). Compare those relationships with those relating to the emphasized notes in measures 7–11 (they are chord tones).

As hinted at on page 64, using just chord tones is perhaps the most obvious and surefire way to make the changes, which is what is done here.

Obvious and surefire, however, are not the foremost traits of a great bebop solo. Chord tones and arpeggios are indeed crucial to making the changes, but you'd find yourself pretty limited if they were all you had in your change-making toolbox.

Making the Changes: Rhythm

The techniques on pages 66–75 will enhance your ability to make the changes, but first we must examine the role of rhythm—specifically, the effect a note's rhythmic placement will have on the harmonic strength of that note.

Strongest   In a measure of $\frac{4}{4}$, the first beat stands out as the most harmonically significant in the measure. Not coincidentally, the chords most frequently change on the first beat of a measure.

If you divide the bar in half, you end up with a note on beat 3 as well on the downbeat. Aside from the downbeat, beat 3 is the next strongest beat in $\frac{4}{4}$, and it's common for chords to change on this beat.

Important chord changes on beats 2 and 4 are fairly infrequent. Note that the rhythmic importance of these beats (for example, their roles in the backbeat) is not to be confused with their harmonic impact.

Weakest   Offbeats are even less harmonically significant, and any further subdivisions of the beat become less important still. Chord changes virtually never occur on the offbeats. Again, be sure not to confuse the role of offbeats in syncopation with their harmonic significance.

Where a note falls within the hierarchy explained above determines its effect in helping to make the changes. It's also important to be able to emphasize the chords at the moments that they change, but even that will generally coincide with this hierarchy. To summarize: A chord tone placed in a "strong" position will help outline the changes, while a clashing non-chord tone with the same rhythmic placement will obscure the changes. Chord tones on weak beats have less harmonic strength. This does not mean that you must play only chord tones on strong beats and save all other notes for weaker beats. When you need to emphasize a chord, however, you'll make significant use of this knowledge.

Note that an anticipation (or any other syncopated note not immediately followed by another note), while adding important rhythmic variety, will have the same harmonic impact as if it landed squarely on the beat that it is anticipating. If in doubt about this, pay attention to the context. A chord tone on a weak beat may actually be functioning as an anticipation to the following strong beat—if the note in question is tied over to the strong beat or if that strong beat is "unoccupied," then you are most likely observing this phenomenon in action. Example 135A shows notes that have the most rhythmic impact because of their rhythmic placement (marked with asterisks). Example 135B shows what happens when some notes are used as anticipations, thus attaining rhythmic emphasis.

The F is implied as an anticipation
as it is the last note heard before the rest.

THE SKELETON OF A BEBOP LINE: GUIDE TONES AND MORE

The essence of a melodic line can often be defined by a small percentage of the notes in that line—a melodic *skeleton*. In fact, it's often only a few notes in a line that determine whether or not that line is making the changes, the remaining notes providing melodic enhancement. Guide tones (see page 61) are a great example of this phenomenon; just two notes outline the sound of one chord moving to the next, and a melodic line is built around that skeleton. That skeleton can also be altered if, for example, you want to change where points of resolution occur. As with arpeggios, the effect of the skeletal notes will be heard most clearly if those notes occur at the moment the chords change.

Another way to achieve this effect is through rhythmic emphasis. If guide tones are emphasized rhythmically (for example, by placing them on stronger beats), they'll stand out.

Yet another way to make guide tones to stand out is through the *register* (the range of notes used) of a line. The ear naturally hears the highest and lowest notes in a line as standing out a bit from others in between. If the peaks and valleys of the line coincide with the guide tones, they will stand out accordingly.

These techniques work not only for guide tones that move from the 7th of one chord to the 3rd of the next, but also for any notes that you choose to emphasize. If you want the sort of focus in your line that comes from a simple melody but also want the excitement of a more involved line, these techniques provide a great compromise. In a sense, you're using some of the same techniques you use in melodic embellishment, except you choose the melody yourself. Play example 139, which uses "Three Blind Mice" as the basis for a bebop line.

This skeletal process is also a way to access the sound of altered dominant chords. The sound of an altered tone resolving to an unaltered note in the chord of resolution, even if a color tone, is a powerful one and contributes to the tension and release central to making the changes.

Example 141 contains the first 16 bars of a popular set of standard changes in the style of the tune "All God's Chillun Got Rhythm" and used for such bop tunes as Bennie Harris's "Reets and I," Miles Davis's "Little Willie Leaps" and Horace Silver's "May-Reh." This example includes a skeleton of important change-making notes that you could use to negotiate these changes.

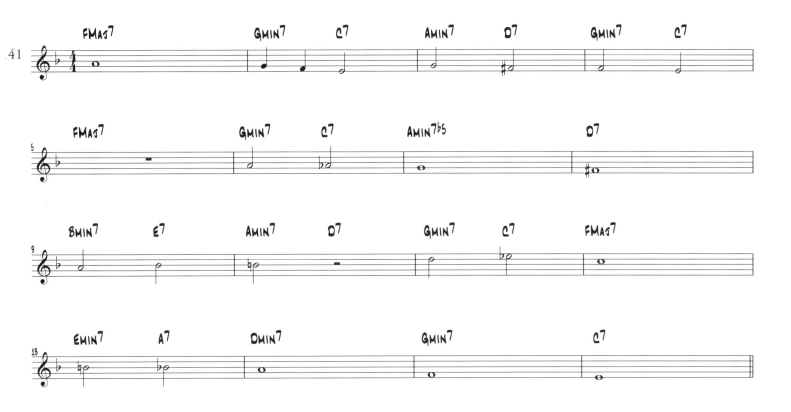

Example 142 takes the same changes and the same skeleton and shows how you might flesh out the skeleton from example 141 into a full-fledged bebop improvisation.

Using Modes to Make the Changes

Using a single scale through a whole progression is fine, but it doesn't always lend itself to making the changes. On the other hand, using chord tones solves that problem but makes it more difficult to create a lyrical melody. In a sense, using modes over individual chords in a progression gives you the best of both worlds. You get a lot of the melodic flexibility of scales and the change-making properties of chord tones in one technique. Check out example 143, which uses the mode that relates to each chord within the key (F Major).

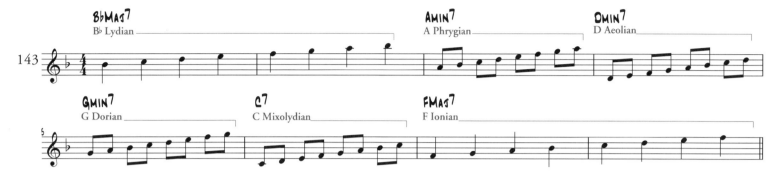

Once you practice the modes "straight" on any changes, you can begin to do so with more flexibility—that is, in a real melodic context.

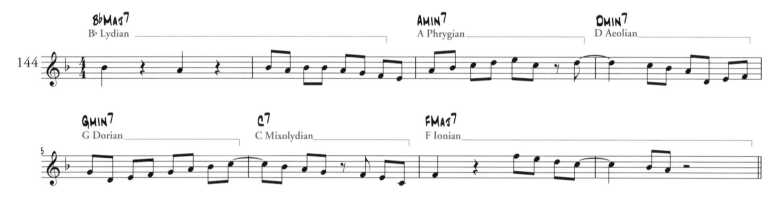

Jazz musicians often choose modes other than those dictated by the diatonic harmony. For example, the prevalence of the ♯11 as a color tone for a Maj7 chord leads many players to use the Lydian mode on a Maj7, even when it is not the IV chord in the key.

Likewise, minor-key progressions can present similar choices. For one thing, the Locrian mode can be applied to a min7♭5 chord regardless of context (Chapters 5 and 6 will provide more options for this chord). The Dorian mode is used on tonic minor chords (that is, minor chords that function as i) even more often than Aeolian, which may seem to be the more logical choice.

Example 147 is a sample solo chorus that uses modes. The changes are in the style of those in the standard "My Shining Hour," a tune that has been recorded by such jazz stars as Count Basie and John Coltrane, as well as by less famous folks like the great pianists Larry Willis, Bruce Barth and Geoff Keezer. Notice that while the expected (that is, diatonic) modes are used for the most part, this example also includes more colorful possibilities, such as the Dorian in measure 9 and the Lydian in measures 19 and 31.

USING ORNAMENTS AND CHROMATIC NOTES

One of the reasons for using an ornament in any sense is not only to "dress up," but also to draw attention to the object being ornamented. For example, a brightly-colored pair of earrings will draw attention to a person's face. In music, ornamentation is a way of not only decorating, but also emphasizing a note. Ornaments are useful in many situations for the expressive quality they can bring to a note—something that comes in handy in the act of making the changes. If one of the main goals is to effectively emphasize the sound of certain notes, particularly chord tones, ornaments provide a series of tools to help do just that.

♩ = Emphasized note

Adding chromatic notes to the mix greatly enhances the palette of available colors. Since chromatic notes tend to create more tension than diatonic notes, they draw even more attention to the main note, and a powerful landing on the main note in turn resolves all that tension.

Feel free to experiment with ornaments and with mixing diatonic and chromatic notes.

Chromatic passing tones have the additional benefit of providing a sort of bridge between diatonic notes. If, for example, you have a series of successive diatonic notes (example 150A) and want to have more of an edge to the line, using chromatic passing tones can be a perfect solution (example 150B); just make sure that you play the rhythms in a way that makes clear which tones are which.

Diatonic Passage   With Added Chromatic Passing Tones

Bebop scales are a good example of the way in which chromatic passing tones can help build change-making lines. The chromatic passing tone between the 1 and ♭7 makes every other note a chord tone, so if you begin on an onbeat and play an eighth-note line, each subsequent onbeat will be a chord tone. The scale is traditionally preceded by an ascending arpeggio and played in a descending motion.

The sample solo chorus in example 152 shows ornaments and chromatic devices in action. The changes are in the style of those Clifford Brown used as changes in his solo for his classic tune "Joy Spring." Clifford's playing continues to be deeply admired, and his change-making abilities, including his use of both diatonic and chromatic ornamentation, was phenomenal.

SUBSTITUTION AS AN IMPROVISATIONAL TOOL

The techniques we've been exploring provide numerous ways to negotiate the increasingly advanced sorts of changes you'll encounter when you delve deeper into the jazz repertoire. Dominant cycles, tritone substitution, unpredictable modulations and turning dominant 7th chords into ii–V's are some of the devices that appear in jazz tunes and that one must be able to negotiate when playing these tunes. Having this mastery also gives you the freedom to spontaneously apply substitution to your improvisation by deriving the content of your solo line from substitute changes. As a rule, the chords of resolution should generally be left alone, but the laws of tension and release allow you to take liberties with the chords that precede them. Even if the rhythm section does not follow you, the tension is taken care of as everyone lands simultaneously on a chord of resolution, and it still sounds like you are making the changes.

Substitution in a solo can occur with or without the reinforcement of the left hand. In other words, you can either play the substitutions in your left hand to reinforce the changes upon which your solo line is based, or you can play the original changes in your left hand to emphasize the tension that is to be resolved. Some of the reasons for using substitutions in a solo are:

• The chord progression is fairly static, and you want to add more motion and stimulation.

• You want to intensify the tension and release leading to a particular chord of resolution.

• You are playing multiple choruses on a tune, and the act of trying to make the changes is leading you to repeat material, so you want to vary the changes to generate varied melodies.

Having looked at the *reasons* for using substitutions, let's look at a few examples of *how*. Let's say we have an ordinary ii–V–I in the key of B♭ Major.

Using techniques like those we reviewed on page 59, here are a number of ways you could use substitutions to create lines. Note that the changes shown are implied by the lines.

As you can hear, some of these substitutions are very intense and far removed from the ii–V from which they originated. So, proceed with caution, reserving more intense and dissonant substitutions for moments where such intensity and dissonance are appropriate.

On this page you'll find a sample one-chorus solo over *Rhythm changes*. These changes, originally used in Gershwin's "I Got Rhythm," are second only to the blues in their prevalence in jazz. Great jazz tunes based on Rhythm changes include "Lester Leaps In," "Cottontail," "The Theme," "Anthropology," "Moose the Mooche," "Dexterity," "Oleo," "Rhythm-A-Ning" and countless others. Rhythm changes also serve often as the basis for tunes that make significant use of substitutions, such as "Room 608," "The Eternal Triangle," "Brownie Speaks," "C.T.A." and "Humph." The sample solo below uses a great deal of substitution. The changes closest to the staff are the classic Rhythm changes, which would be played by the rhythm section; the changes in gray reflect the substitutions implied by the solo line.

MAKING THE CHANGES: PUTTING IT TOGETHER

Each of the change-making techniques we've looked at should be practiced separately for maximum reinforcement. But a well-constructed solo uses a combination of devices. Example 153 combines these change-making techniques, here applied to one chorus of soloing. The changes are in the style of those for the Ray Noble standard "Cherokee," one of the most commonly played tunes in jazz, especially in a bebop setting. Note the long (64-measure) form. Implied substitutions, shown in gray, appear above the core harmonies.

You're encouraged to apply these change-making techniques to as many tunes and chord progressions as possible, using all 12 keys. The greater the number of different sets of changes you've practiced soloing over, the less likely you'll be caught off guard in a tune.

CONCEPTUAL CORNER:
EXTREMES OF TEMPO—BALLADS AND BURNERS

Most of the information in this book is relevant to improvisation at any tempo; after all, a G7 is a G7 no matter where you set the metronome. However, that doesn't mean that any approach to creating lines is equally appropriate to any tempo. In this Conceptual Corner, we'll explore some topics related to improvising at tempos that are especially fast or slow. Exactly how fast is fast? How slow is slow? There's no clear-cut answer to these questions. From a practical standpoint, it depends on the individual.

In the days before bebop, most ballads and fast numbers fit into what would now be defined as a medium tempo, as it would have been too difficult to dance to slower ballads or brighter fast numbers. With the dawn of the bebop era and a shift from danceable jazz to a more listener-oriented, "art music" approach, extremes of tempo became much more pronounced. Artists like Charlie Parker and Bud Powell began to play very slow ballads and burning, up-tempo numbers; and the ability to play at these tempos became essential for jazz musicians. Since then, some musicians have taken extremes of tempo to startling levels. For our purposes, just remember that fast and slow are by nature relative terms, so their exact definitions will depend on your skills, your tastes and the habits of the people with whom you play.

Playing at a Slow Tempo: Ballads

You could devote an entire book to the nuances and different approaches involved in playing ballads. If you were to survey a number of skilled, seasoned jazz musicians, you would likely discover that they consider playing slow tempos to be more challenging than playing fast ones. This statement may seem counterintuitive to anybody who is still working to develop the technique and fluency necessary to play at a bright tempo, but there is a lot of truth to it. In spite of the technical challenges a fast tune presents, the momentum can, to a certain extent, take on a life of its own. Assuming you have the chops to handle the tune and are feeling locked into the beat, you can surf through the tune, riding a high-energy wave. A very slow tune requires far less technique, assuming that one thinks of technique as being synonymous with dexterity. However, a slow tune requires a far different sort of concentration, restraint and maturity. It is no accident that older, more experienced musicians are often the ones most revered for their ability to play a convincing ballad. While maturity isn't a skill, nor can it be practiced, there are some tips and techniques that can help you make a ballad more convincing, as well as help you avoid some of the common pitfalls.

Any player of ballads must become comfortable with space and silence. A skilled ballad player does not fill every beat of every measure with sound. One of the biggest challenges is allowing a note to sit and be followed by silence. It's a vulnerable feeling for the player, but one that's essential to being able to play lyrically. Learn to control the instinct to keep playing until you find the "right" note. Another important tool for playing a slow ballad is learning the lyrics. Knowing the words to a song greatly helps one's phrasing and connection to the meaning of a song. In fact, many old-school ballad masters would scoff at the very idea of playing a ballad without taking the time to know the lyrics. Obviously, this doesn't apply to modern jazz ballads that don't have lyrics. On a stylistic note, also keep in mind that jazz ballads, especially slower ones, are often played with straight eighths.

On the subject of pitfalls, there are two that stand out. The first is playing too many notes. An inexperienced ballad player will sometimes react to the slow pace of the changes by trying to cram in as many notes as possible. Of course, plenty of great ballad players use a lot of notes; just listen to Art Tatum. So, how many notes are too many? Ask yourself the following question when playing a lot of notes on a ballad: "Am I doing it out of technical self-indulgence, or because I sincerely feel that the line expresses something?" The second notable pitfall is simply getting lost. A slower tempo and a subtler groove provide plenty of opportunities for losing concentration. One lapse of focus, and you might "wake up" not knowing where you are in the tune. The solution is to work on increasing your ability to focus and expanding your attention span.

Playing at a Fast Tempo: Burners

The biggest misconception about playing fast tunes is that the main challenge is to have the dexterity (or "chops") to play a lot of notes in a short period of time. While there are indeed technical challenges on fast tunes, the main challenge is more mental than physical. To play fast tunes, it's absolutely essential to be able to feel and keep track of the pulse while remaining completely relaxed. There is a difference between playing fast lines and playing fast tunes; sometimes both happen simultaneously, but not always. You may have noticed that it's often easier to double up (play double-time-type figures) on a slow tune than it is to play normal eighth-note lines on a fast tune, even if the number of notes played per second is identical. That's because a slower tune presents fewer challenges with keeping the pulse. When the beat is brisk, it's crucial that the notes land in places that are rhythmically consistent with the groove.

Someone who is uneasy with playing at a given tempo is likely to tense up in response to this challenge, which makes it nearly impossible to get in the groove. This tension often arises from a player's fear that he or she doesn't have the chops to keep up. There have been numerous jazz legends—Thelonious Monk, Miles Davis, J. J. Johnson and Wes Montgomery, to name a few—who for whatever reason did not or could not play lines as fast as those played by people like Charlie Parker or Bud Powell. Yet these players all sounded not only great, but also completely at ease on fast tunes. Remember that the key is not necessarily to play a lot of notes, but for whatever notes you do play to be in the pocket.

The technical aspect should not be neglected entirely, of course. Being comfortable with the beat is the number-one concern, because no amount of chops will keep you from sounding ill at ease if you are, in fact, ill at ease. Still, you should also work on the technical side of a tune in order to maximize creative flow. Depending on the tune and on your tastes, this may involve anything from brushing up your familiarity with the changes to an exhaustive examination of the melodic and harmonic possibilities of the tune, a 12-key workout and so on. It's simply a result of physics that if the tempo is faster, you'll have less time to think. Therefore, being in technical control will invariably free up more of your brain for spontaneity and creativity. Meanwhile, relaxation and rhythmic ease are difficult to attain if you're not technically fluent with the tune. As we've noted, that fluency will take on a different form for someone playing in the style of Thelonious Monk than it will for a chops-fiend in the Oscar Peterson mold. But if you have ever played a tune that you can't quite handle, then you know how tense a situation that is and must realize how that tension inhibits you, whatever your style.

The way to tackle the challenge of playing fast tunes is to take it a little bit at a time, a method that is essentially no different from how you should tackle any jazz challenge. If you begin by cranking up the metronome to 40 bpm (beats per minute) past the point you can handle comfortably, it's unlikely to do anything but frustrate you, unless you're genuinely curious to see how you measure up at that tempo. Practice at a tempo that's comfortable for you, and increase the metronome's speed one notch at a time. You'll likely notice a gray area, where you can still handle it, though it's becoming more of a struggle. Pinpoint that zone of tempos until your comfort level increases and your gray area is faster. You can, of course, repeat this ad infinitum, until your comfort level is scorchingly fast.

As for the metronome, there are different opinions about how to use it. Few people deny that the metronome is an essential tool for working on fast tunes. After all, how else are you going to insure that you're keeping up? One issue that arises is which beats the metronome should outline. Most metronomes go up only to 208 bpm, and you're unlikely to be able to have a beat on each quarter note once you get into the fast-o-sphere. For that matter, having quarter notes beating at 300 bpm would be rather distracting. The options that remain are beats 1 and 3, or beats 2 and 4. Assuming that we're dealing with swing feel, some would say that you absolutely must use beats 2 and 4 to maintain the feeling of swing and the presence of a backbeat. In practice, though, this can be challenging to the point of being cumbersome. If you try it this way and discover that you're losing the beat or turning it around, switch to 1 and 3. You can always switch back once you're more comfortable. Also, the groove is not sacrificed in the same way on a very fast tune, as the bright tempo changes the very nature of the backbeat.

THE BLUES

Jazz, since its inception, has been rooted in the blues. Some would say that without a perceptible level of blues influence, music can't legitimately be called jazz. Whether or not you're of that opinion, there's no denying that the blues is central to the study and history of jazz. The 12-bar blues form is inescapable in virtually any form of jazz. A great deal of the phrasing and some of the vocabulary of jazz comes from the blues. Virtually all of the most admired musicians in the history of jazz, from Jelly Roll Morton to Count Basie to Charlie Parker to Ornette Coleman, have had a deep love for and deep roots in the blues.

The devices shown on page 60 are useful, but only insofar as you can make them reflect a true blues feeling. This feeling can only be credibly approached by someone who has listened to enough blues (or other music with strong blues roots) to understand the sound and phrasing. If you have a background in this sort of music, you may already be well equipped. If you need to do some remedial blues listening, here are a few keyboardists you might want to check out:

Boogie-Woogie: Meade Lux Lewis, Albert Ammons, Pete Johnson, Peetie Wheatstraw

Chicago Style: Big Maceo Merriweather, Otis Spann, Pinetop Perkins, Sunnyland Slim

New Orleans Style: Professor Longhair, James Booker, Katie Webster, Clifton Chenier

At the same time, don't limit yourself to keyboard players. Much of the blues keyboard vocabulary is built around trying to make the piano simulate the expressive bends and moans of the voice, guitar and harp (aka harmonica or mouth harp). Some non-keyboard greats to check out:

Vocals: Bessie Smith, Ma Rainey, Koko Taylor, Etta James, Jimmy Reed, Howlin' Wolf

Vocals and Guitar: Robert Johnson, Big Bill Broonzy, Blind Lemon Jefferson, T-Bone Walker, B.B. King, Muddy Waters, John Lee Hooker, Elmore James, Lightnin' Hopkins, Buddy Guy

Harp: Little Walter, Junior Wells, James Cotton, Sonny Boy Williamson, Big Walter Horton

These lists do not include influential blues artists poorly represented on recordings, such as Clarence "Pine Top" Smith, nor do they include the many great jazz musicians who have been influenced by the blues. Of course, the blues is present in most jazz musicians' styles; even artists like Lennie Tristano and John Lewis displayed deep and convincing roots in the blues, though their music tends to be associated with more cerebral jazz styles. That said, some players have made more explicit use of blues phrasing and vocabulary. These musicians are often categorized (fairly or not) as "soul-jazz" players. Post-bebop pianists whose playing styles are inexorably linked to the blues include Ray Charles, Bobby Timmons, Junior Mance, Ramsey Lewis, Gene Harris and Les McCann. Organists in the same category include Jimmy Smith, Jimmy McGriff, Richard "Groove" Holmes and Charles Earland.

In addition to internalizing the phrasing and inflections of the blues, one must learn to make judicious use of *blue notes*. From an aesthetic point of view, a blue note is a note that is inflected with blues feeling, often by flatting it, bending it or smearing it downward. From a theoretical point of view, there are different opinions of what exactly constitutes a blue note. Three specific scale degrees— $\flat$3, $\flat$5 and $\flat$7—are generally understood as "blue," especially when contrasted against their "natural" forms in a scale or chord. The blues scale, which we looked at on page 10, manages to get all three blue notes into one scale, which helps explain both its name and its popularity. Some players use blue notes all the time, while others use them only rarely. Whatever your taste for blue notes, you're encouraged to become comfortable with them. This will require relaxing your diligence in applying some of the principles you've learned in making the changes, since blue notes often stand out in sharp relief to notes that outline the chords.

So, when is it appropriate to bust out with your bluest blues? You must consider you own style, as well as that of the band. Les McCann, for example, might "blue it up" at any time, while Herbie Hancock might be more selective in choosing which repertoire was most suited to gritty blues playing. Some standards lend themselves more naturally to greasy blues treatment than others do. A tune with complex harmonies, for example, can be difficult to play this way, since the simplicity and earthiness of the blues may not sync up with all those changes. Harmonically simpler tunes, on the other hand, can be perfect. Minor-key tunes hold up well under this treatment, since the blues scale, with its ♭3 and ♭7, fits neatly into minor keys. Example 157 shows the application of a blues approach to changes in the style of those in the A section of the popular standard "Alone Together."

Of course, the most obvious place to play in a blues style is on a blues tune. Example 158 uses one chorus of a basic 12-bar blues progression in B♭.

Of course, incorporating the feeling of the blues isn't a simple "yes or no" proposition. Charlie Parker recorded very few songs with as overt a blues-based approach as that on the classic "Parker's Mood," yet even his most dexterous up-tempo numbers reflected a deep blues feeling and moments of blues-inspired phrasing. Among pianists, Horace Silver is similarly renowned for the blues feeling in even his most beboppin' lines. You're encouraged to let your use of the blues run its natural course based on your own tastes and the musical situation at hand. If, for example, you encounter a typical bebop-inspired blues like that on page 49, you have several options. You can make it as down-home as you would a more basic blues, play it as you would any other tune with a lot of dominant chords (using, for example, the Mixolydian mode and the bebop scale) or find a middle ground. Example 159 does the last of these, using a combination of blues and bop.

Example 160 is a sample chorus in the style of "Bird Blues," a complex blues progression favored by Charlie Parker, who used it in his landmark "Blues For Alice." Similar changes can be found in Bud Powell's "Dance of the Infidels" and Miles Davis's "Sippin' At Bells." Note that the complexity of changes limits the ease with which you can apply blues devices.

Another type of blues progression is the minor blues, the basis for such modern jazz landmarks as Dizzy Gillespie's "Birk's Works," Oliver Nelson's "Stolen Moments," John Coltrane's "Mr. P. C." and Wayne Shorter's "Footprints." The first 12 bars of example 158 demonstrate a chorus on a B♭ Minor blues approached from a bebop-oriented change-making perspective. The next 12 bars are a blues-drenched chorus on the same minor blues. As you play, note the differences between these two sections.

Some of the musicians best known for their ability to go from change-making bop to gutbucket blues include saxophonists Yusef Lateef, Eddie Harris and Rahsaan Roland Kirk, trumpeters Lee Morgan, Freddie Hubbard and Booker Little, vibraphonist Milt Jackson and bassist Charles Mingus. Keyboard greats known for this kind of dual personality include Oscar Peterson, Don Patterson, Hampton Hawes, Wynton Kelly, Phineas Newborn, Jr. and Ray Bryant.

CONCEPTUAL CORNER:
INSPIRATION FROM OTHER SOURCES

Q: True or false: To play just like Bud Powell, you should listen only to recordings of Bud Powell.

A: False

The seeming paradox above really isn't that contradictory. After all, Bud Powell himself was checking out everyone from Art Tatum to J. S. Bach, which is a lot broader than just listening to Bud Powell. So, if you listen only to him, your ability to emulate him will be limited. If your goal *isn't* to be an exact replica of him (or of any other artist), it becomes that much clearer that a broader palette of influences will serve you well.

The blues have influenced nearly every jazz pianist and organist, a phenomenon that we've just examined in some depth. But what about other styles? There are countless examples of jazz pianists who have been strongly influenced by other styles. Western classical music has been a great source of influence to many. Baroque keyboard music, like that of J. S. Bach, has had a noticeable impact on artists from John Lewis to Keith Jarrett. Artists like Herbie Hancock have borrowed a great deal from Romantic and French impressionist composers such as Debussy. Many pianists, especially those in the avant-garde jazz scene, have drawn inspiration from modern composers in the 20th-century classical idiom, including Stravinsky and Bartók.

R&B and gospel styles have found their way into the concepts of modern jazz pianists like James Williams, Les McCann and Ray Bryant. Meanwhile, the majority of the giants of the organ have also been affected by these styles. With the steady popularity of rock 'n' roll since the 1960s, a staggering number of jazz artists have at least dabbled in the repertoire and/or rhythms of rock and pop. For example, literally dozens of Stevie Wonder's tunes have been recorded in straight-ahead jazz settings. Further, none of this even addresses the vast world of jazz-rock fusion.

As jazz has become more and more international, more and more of what we call "world music" has entered into the jazz language, sometimes at the hands of people connected to those cultures, sometimes at the hands of musicians who are simply curious. Randy Weston and Abdullah Ibrahim (aka Dollar Brand) have developed jazz piano styles rooted in African music. Toshiko Akiyoshi and Sumi Tonooka are among those who have incorporated traditional Japanese music. Latin music has been a significant influence on many non-Latin musicians, from Jelly Roll Morton to George Shearing to Mark Levine. Meanwhile, Latin American pianists like Danilo Perez, Hilton Ruiz and Gonzalo Rubalcaba have shown themselves to be equally well schooled in Latin music and modern straight-ahead jazz. Other players, like Ran Blake and Joe Zawinul, have explored and incorporated diverse styles of folk music from around the world.

Another way to open up your ears is to make a point of listening to other instruments. Granted, anybody could spend a lifetime examining the work of great jazz pianists and organists without running out of material. That said, many of those artists' innovations came from working to emulate other instruments. Erroll Garner, for example, often strummed chords with his left hand in a style that evoked the guitar. Cecil Taylor's rhythmic playing often shows him to be as much a percussionist as a pianist. From the early heyday of Jimmy Smith to the present, most organists have worked on bass lines inspired by the great double bassists of jazz. Since the 1920s and the rise to prominence of pianist Earl Hines, keyboard players have often tried to emulate horns and vocalists with right-hand solo lines. Horn players like Louis Armstrong, Charlie Parker and John Coltrane have exerted such a strong influence that studying their playing is virtually inevitable. Many great non-keyboardists have done things worth checking out, and these things can be the source of great substance in your own playing. From the rhythmic punch of Art Blakey's drumming to the wailing passion of Sidney Bechet's phrasing on the clarinet, you're bound to benefit from broadening your sphere of listening. This influence has also worked in the other direction, as pianists like Powell, Monk and Tatum have influenced countless other musicians in one way or another.

The moral is this: Listen to everything you can. Listen to all styles of music. If you like it, see how it fits into your concept. If you don't like it, check it out anyway, if only to open your mind. Listen to drummers and bassists, to horn players and vocalists: anyone with something to say. Having broad personal tastes and influences is inspiring and will add depth to your playing.

PACING

"You're not going to believe this, I have something really exciting to say!"

Try saying the above sentence, enunciating each word loudly and at the same volume and pitch, with the syllables spaced evenly ("YOU'RE NOT GO-ING TO BE-LIEVE…"). In spite of the intriguing message, this will sound obnoxious, not exciting. Now, try saying the same sentence the way you might actually say it if you were communicating a great piece of news. Notice how you instinctively change your volume level, speed up and slow down and so on. The force of your communication depends largely on the way you pace your delivery of the words.

So it goes in music. We've spent the bulk of this chapter acquiring tools and language, but now, let's talk for a moment about using that language to communicate. Lester Young is credited with the sage advice to "tell a story" when playing a solo. One of the most effective ways to do this is through pacing. A good solo, like a good story, varies in intensity, often building over time. While not every solo must progress predictably from a whisper to a scream, it is vitally important to be conscious of the pacing in one's solos and to develop the ability to control it. Even a mundane line can be powerful if it represents a jump in intensity from whatever came before. In this way, pacing is as important as language in communicating with listeners. Of course, if a solo is well paced and the lines aren't mundane, that's when the music really cooks.

Here are some of the most crucial elements in pacing a solo.

- **Number of notes:** As a rule, a line or phrase with more notes is more intense than one with fewer, so longer phrases and more notes can up the ante of intensity. Just as importantly, a "normal" phrase will seem more intense if it follows sparser playing with a lot of space and silence.

- **Rhythmic intensity:** Sometimes this is synonymous with number of notes, in that the more notes you cram into a span of time, the more rhythmic intensity you're likely to create. Still, you can create rhythmic intensity in other ways. Increased unpredictability and/or syncopation, for example, can have an intensifying effect. Note also that while an increase in the sheer number of notes increases the density of sound, it will not always increase the rhythmic intensity. A stream of constant sixteenth notes is often less intense than a varied eighth-note line. On page 123, we'll examine some other ways of increasing rhythmic intensity.

- **Dissonance:** A common and effective way to build intensity is through an increase in the amount of dissonance. While much of Chapters 5 and 6 are devoted to tools that provide an even greater amount of dissonance, there are already a number of tools at your disposal to bring about this effect. For example, chord tones are as consonant as consonant can be. Adding other scale tones introduces more dissonance. Adding chromatic notes (through the use of ornaments or as altered tones in dominant 7th chords) creates still more dissonance.

- **Dynamics:** If you've ever yelled, you know that loud tends to be more dramatic than soft, and this is important to remember when pacing a solo. Also important to remember is that contrast (mixing up loud and soft) can be a dramatic and intense device.

- **Range:** The increase in a solo line's range (making the highs higher and/or the lows lower) can be an effective intensity-building device, much like a low growl or dramatic high note that you sometimes hear from a vocalist in a climactic moment. With some instruments, particularly wind instruments, there is a distinct change in timbre when the higher or lower register is used. With the keyboard, one must be sensitive to the individual instrument. A dramatic, screaming high note on the organ, for example, can be ground-shaking. On a piano, the same note may be dramatic, or it may be tinny and wimpy, depending on the instrument.

- **Special Devices:** Each instrument has special idiomatic devices that are inherently intense, from a bent note on a guitar to a half-valved smear on a trumpet. On a keyboard, these devices include octaves, tremolos and other blues techniques—devices whose very nature is to create intensity. On page 120, we'll look at a few other such devices.

- **Passion:** This is an intangible but undeniable element in building intensity. As essential as the above elements may be, they will not have much effect unless played with a sincere passion that reflects the intensity you are trying to project. By the same token, if you lose yourself in passion, these things may come out naturally as you play. If you've practiced thoroughly, you can let your passion guide you on the path to maximum intensity.

The changes used in examples 162 and 163 are in the style of those in the popular jazz tune "Four," alternately credited to Miles Davis and Eddie "Cleanhead" Vinson. Great versions of that tune have been recorded by many other jazz artists, including Sonny Rollins, Phineas Newborn, Jr. and Joe Henderson, and more recent versions by pianists Mulgrew Miller, Bill Mays, Rob Schneiderman, Norman Simmons, Duke Jordan and Gonzalo Rubalcaba. Example 162 is a chorus in the spacious, restrained style that might be appropriate for the early part of a solo.

Example 163 is another chorus using the same changes as in example 162. This chorus has a lot more notes, a broader range, more non-diatonic colors and a more intense rhythm. This version is an example of what you might play later in the same solo, after having built up some momentum.

Of course, everyone has a different sense of pacing and a different range of intensity that feels satisfying. The ultimate goals are to be conscious and in control of the way the pacing unfolds, and to play with the utmost efficiency. Efficiency—of touch, dynamic, rhythm and so on—is crucial at both ends of the intensity spectrum. When playing sparsely, every note counts and needs to be played with focus and clarity for the clearest communication. When playing a lot of notes, efficient playing ensures that your lines won't become nonsense. Diligent practice is the key to efficiency. Performance time is when you want to be spontaneous and in the moment, so the bandstand is not the place to be thinking about efficiency. Work on this as you practice, so your playing can be *naturally* focused and efficient.

MORE SCALES: MELODIC MINOR AND ITS MODES

We've already explored two of the three main forms of the minor scale, natural minor and harmonic minor. The third form, the *melodic minor*, uses ♭3 when it ascends, and ♭3, ♭6 and ♭7 when it descends.

The ♮6 and ♮7 in the ascending form help lead you to 1 (as in major), while the ♭7 and ♭6 in the descending form (as in natural minor) help lead you to 5. In jazz, only the ascending form of the scale is used, in which case it can be called *jazz melodic minor*.

As with the major scale, you can derive modes from melodic minor by beginning on each degree. These modes have descriptive names.

1st Mode: C Melodic Minor (aka Jazz Melodic Minor)

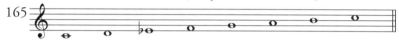

2nd Mode: D Dorian ♭2   3rd Mode: E♭ Lydian Augmented

4th Mode: F Lydian ♭7 (aka Lydian Dominant)   5th Mode: G Mixolydian ♭6

6th Mode: A Locrian ♮2   7th Mode: B Altered (aka Super Locrian)

Modes of Melodic Minor as Autonomous Scales

As with the modes of the major scale, the modes of melodic minor can and should be learned as scales unto themselves. Each mode implies not only a chord, but specific color tones as well. For example, three modes imply dominant 7th chords, but each with different colors.

Mode	Numeric Formula	Chord Implied	Chord Colors Implied
Melodic Minor	1, 2, ♭3, 4, 5, 6, 7, 1	min/Maj7 (or min6)	9, 11, 13(6)
Dorian ♭2	1, ♭2, ♭3, 4, 5, 6, ♭7, 1	min7 (or min6)	♭9, 11
Lydian Augmented	1, 2, 3, ♯4, ♯5, 6, 7, 1	Maj7♯5	9, ♯11, 13
Lydian ♭7	1, 2, 3, ♯4, 5, 6, ♭7, 1	Dominant 7	9, ♯11, 13
Mixolydian ♭6	1, 2, 3, 4, 5, ♭6, ♭7, 1	Dominant 7	9, 11(4), ♭13(♯5)
Locrian ♯2	1, 2, ♭3, 4, ♭5, ♭6, ♭7, 1	min7♭5	9, 11
Altered	1, 2, ♭3, 3, ♭5, ♭6, ♭7, 1	Dominant 7	♭9, ♯9, ♭5, ♯5

Here are the seven modes of melodic minor, all starting on C. As with the modes of the major scale, learn and practice each mode beginning on all 12 tonic notes, one mode at a time. Where the scale degree differs from that of the major scale, the alteration is shown.

MORE SCALES: HARMONIC MINOR SCALE AND ITS MODES

Wee learned about the harmonic minor scale on page 10, so now we can extract its modes as we have with the other scales we've looked at. Unlike the modes of the major and melodic minor scales, the modes that are used most often, the modes of harmonic minor do not have names, only numbers according to the beginning scale degree. The harmonic minor scale itself is called the 1st mode; the mode beginning on the 2nd scale degree is called the 2nd mode of harmonic minor; and so on. The key is not what to call it, but how you can use it.

C Harmonic Minor 1st Mode

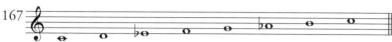

2nd Mode

3rd Mode

4th Mode

5th Mode

6th Mode

7th Mode

Modes of Harmonic Minor as Autonomous Scales

Let's look at the formula and the chordal implications for each of the harmonic minor modes. In this chart, most of the "chord colors implied" are those you would typically find in a chord of that type. Don't let that deter you, though, from experimenting with the other colors!

MODE	NUMERIC FORMULA	CHORD IMPLIED	CHORD COLORS IMPLIED
Harmonic Minor	1, 2, ♭3, 4, 5, ♭6, 7, 1	min/Maj7	9, 11
Mode 2	1, ♭2, ♭3, 4, ♭5, 6, ♭7, 1	min7♭5	11
Mode 3	1, 2, 3, 4, ♯5, 6, 7, 1	Maj7♯5	9, 13
Mode 4	1, 2, ♭3, ♯4, 5, 6, ♭7, 1	min7	9, ♯11
Mode 5	1, ♭2, 3, 4, 5, ♭6, ♭7, 1	Dominant 7	♭9, 11(4), ♭13(♯5)
Mode 6	1, ♯2, 3, ♯4, 5, 6, 7, 1	Maj7	(♯9), ♯11, 13
Mode 7	1, ♭2, ♭3, 3, ♭5, ♭6, ♭♭7, 1	dim7	♭13

Here are the seven modes of the harmonic minor, each starting on C. If you like the sound of any or all of these modes, practice them as you would any other scale.

C Harmonic Minor 1st Mode

MORE SCALES: LYDIAN DIMINISHED SCALE AND ITS MODES

Lydian diminished, a scale not typically found in other styles of music but immensely useful for jazz musicians, is like a Lydian mode with a ♭3. As in the case of harmonic minor, the modes of Lydian diminished are usually identified with numbers rather than names. The exception is the 5th mode, which resembles a harmonic minor scale with a ♮3, thus the name *harmonic major.*

C Lydian Diminished: 1st Mode

162

2nd Mode   3rd Mode

4th Mode   5th Mode (aka Harmonic Major)

6th Mode   7th Mode

Modes of Lydian Diminished as Autonomous Scales

Now that we're used to the autonomous scale drill, let's look at the vital statistics for the Lydian Diminished modes. As with harmonic minor, the chord colors implied are mostly limited to those that you would typically find in a chord of that type, though you're encouraged to explore other colors. Since these modes often imply multiple chords, the "chord colors implied" relate to the first chord listed; these are the most common.

Mode	Numeric Formula	Chord Implied	Chord Colors Implied
Lydian Diminished	1, 2, ♭3, ♯4, 5, 6, 7, 1	min/Maj7–min6–dim7	9, 13(6)
Mode 2	1, ♭2, 3, 4, 5, 6, ♭7, 1	Dominant 7	♭9, 11(4), 13
Mode 3	1, ♯2, 3, ♯4, ♯5, 6, 7, 1	Maj7♯5–dim7	(♯9), ♯11, 13
Mode 4	1, ♭2, ♭3, 4, ♭5, ♭6, ♭♭7, 1	dim7	11, ♭13
Mode 5–Harmonic Major	1, 2, 3, 4, 5, ♭6, 7, 1	Maj7–Maj7♯5	9, ♯5
Mode 6	1, 2, ♭3, 4, ♭5, 6, ♭7, 1	min7♭5	9, 11
Mode 7	1, ♭2, ♭3, 3, 5, ♭6, ♭7, 1	Dominant 7–min7	♭9, ♯9, ♭13(♯5)

Dig into each of the Lydian diminished modes and take them through the different keys, keeping track of the associated chords.

C Lydian Diminished: 1st Mode

170

MORE SCALES: SYMMETRICAL SCALES

A *symmetrical scale* is any scale based on the repetition of a single interval or pattern of intervals. These scales can sound great and their symmetry and regularity simplifies the learning process, since learning any of these scales depends only on remembering the pattern upon which the scale is based. One interesting feature of symmetrical scales is that, unlike major or minor scales, a symmetrical scale built on one note will always have a corresponding scale on another note that will yield the same exact pitches; we'll look at this feature below.

Diminished Scales

The commonly-used symmetrical scales below are most often referred to as *diminished scales*. There are two different types of diminished scales, each made up of alternating half steps and whole steps.

The *half-whole diminished scale* is based on the pattern of a half step followed by a whole step. This scale is typically used with dominant 7th chords.

C Half-Whole Diminished Scale

The *whole-half diminished scale* is typically used with diminished 7th chords. It is based on a pattern of a whole step followed by a half step.

C Whole-Half Diminished Scale

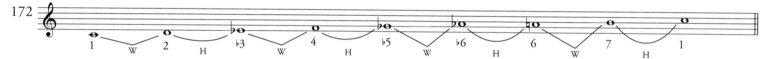

Each of these scales can be seen as a mode of the other. For example, if you begin on the second degree of a whole-half diminished scale, you end up with a half-whole scale. As mentioned above, the symmetry of these scales means that there are only really three different diminished scales of either type. For example, if you build a diminished scale on the third degree of either of the examples we've looked at, the pitches will be exactly the same as those in the original scale. Another way to look at it is that the C, E♭, G♭ and A whole-half diminished scales all use the same eight pitches, as do the D, F, A♭ and B half-whole diminished scales, so that all eight of these scales are modes of one another.

Whole-Tone Scale

The *whole-tone scale* is a six-note scale made up entirely of whole steps. This scale is quite useful with dominant 7th chords (note its prevalence in the solos of Thelonious Monk). Because of their symmetical nature, there are only two different whole-tone scales, one beginning on C, the other on C♯.

C Whole-Tone Scale   C♯ Whole-Tone Scale

It can also be used on tonic minor chords, but only if you use the scale that starts a half step away from the root!

B Whole-Tone Scale

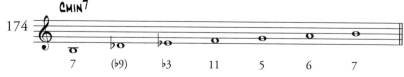

CLUSTERS

The term *cluster* refers to a sonority based on the interval of a 2nd (that is, a whole step or half step), as opposed to triads, which are based on 3rds. The effect of a cluster can vary, but it is invariably intense and striking. Clusters can be used in a context that's funky (Horace Silver, Jimmy Smith), playful (Thelonious Monk, Erroll Garner), jarring (Herbie Nichols, Mal Waldron, Andrew Hill) or *very* jarring (Cecil Taylor, Don Pullen, Myra Melford), not to mention countless possible combinations of these. Clusters are most associated with more avant-garde forms of jazz and are incredibly useful in those contexts, but they can also be used in a purely straight-ahead, harmonically traditional context.

The simplest and perhaps most commonly used form of the cluster is the *harmonic 2nd*. In other words, you simultaneously play two notes a major or minor 2nd apart. If your goal is to stay within the harmony, a number of 2nds will relate well to any given chord. Example 175 shows the harmonic 2nds that work well with CMaj7.

You can also displace one or the other notes in a harmonic 2nd by an octave, which will result in either an *inversion* (a reordering of the interval, explained in further detail on page 109) or a *compound interval* (an interval wider than an octave). Although these are not technically clusters, they are applied in the same ways and in the same contexts as clusters. Notice that while each option in example 176 uses the same two pitches, each has its own color and character.

Harmonic 2nd (M2)   Inversion (m7)   Compound Interval (M9)

Note that on dominant 7th chords, the number of cluster options is even greater because of the possibility for both extensions and altered notes.

You can vary the sound of a cluster by adding notes. Example 177 includes the three-note clusters that relate to CMaj7.

If you want to use more than three notes for a cluster but still want it to relate to the harmony, it's often best to think modally. In other words, think about the scale you'd like to relate to the chord or key center, then build your cluster from a series of notes within that scale. Example 178 shows some multi-note clusters that relate to CMaj7/Lydian.

As previously stated, these examples apply to situations in which you want to adhere to the harmony. Without that restriction, it's purely a matter of texture, rhythm and dynamics. How thick do you want the sound to be? How dissonant? How rhythmically striking? How high or low in register? The only restriction here (again, assuming dissonance isn't inappropriate) is to make sure that you're not bashing the instrument in an abusive way. If the piano strings are snapping, you might want to back off a bit!

LOCKED HANDS

The underrated pianist and organist Milt Buckner is best known for developing a popular style of harmonizing melodies in block chords. The concept is basically orchestral; the piano is used to simulate the effect of a big band's saxophone section. While Buckner's own playing is underrepresented on recordings, his legacy is easy to hear in the pianists who further developed this style. Nat "King" Cole, George Shearing and Red Garland are among those whose variations on this technique have been central to their playing styles. *Locked hands* is the common term for this style of block chord, since it involves moving both hands up and down the keyboard together. It can be used for both playing existing melodies and improvising.

The basis for locked-hands voicing is harmonizing with four-note voicings in *close position*. In this context, close position means that all four of the voices are as close as possible to the melody (top) note, resulting in a voicing with less than an octave between the top and bottom notes. For the purpose of locked hands, you'll want to double the melody note an octave below with the left hand, as shown at right.

Diminished Passing Chords

The other factor that is key to understanding locked hands is the use of *diminished passing chords*, one of the elements derived from big band orchestrations. Logic would seem to dictate that each note in a melody line should be harmonized with the chord that is in effect at that moment. The reality, though, is that doing so tends to produce a harmonically flat sound that is also physically cumbersome. You can create forward motion, however, by harmonizing the passing tones on the weak beats or offbeats with the diminished 7th chord a half step below the main chord. You can also think of this diminished chord as a rootless 7♭9 chord a perfect 5th above the main chord. For example, for a diminished passing chord over a Dmin7, play a rootless, close voicing of A7♭9 (C♯–E–G–B♭, or C♯dim7). Try out example 179 to hear this sound in action. Begin by playing the melody only, then play the harmonized version.

For the sake of easier reading, some of the following examples have the left hand in treble clef, and some use the *8va* in bass clef. These devices avoid excessive ledger lines above a bass clef staff.

The main reason that this sounds good relates to the larger concept of tension and release. The diminished passing chords create tension, which is released each time the main chord returns, thereby keeping things exciting. It doesn't mean, however, that there is necessarily a lot of tension; nobody accuses the Glenn Miller Band of having played music that is excessively tense, and their orchestrations are based on this very concept. In this context, the tense chords go by so fast that the ear hardly has time to perceive any tension. All you hear is motion.

Several variations on locked hands can also be useful. One is to double not only the top note in each voicing, but also the note immediately below, as shown in example 180. This style was used often by Nat "King" Cole.

You can take this idea even further by doubling every note in the right-hand voicing. This technique is best saved for lush passages at slower tempos, in the style of Dr. Billy Taylor.

For a more spread-out, less dense voicing, you can use the *drop-two* approach, in which you take the second highest note in the voicing and move it down an octave. You can hear a good use of drop-two voicings on the recordings of Red Garland.

You can take drop-two voicing a step further with the *drop-two, drop-four*, in which you move the second and fourth notes in the voicing down an octave. This is another technique that works best at slower tempos.

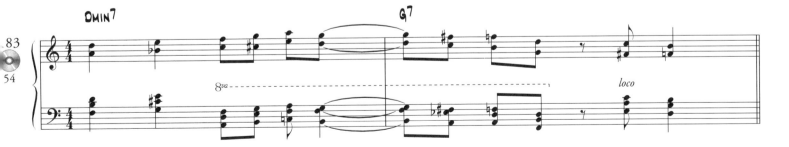

REHARMONIZATION

We've already explored substitution, which involves changing certain chords within a progression in a way that maintains the essence of the original progression. *Reharmonization* takes substitution a step further by fundamentally altering the harmonic structure of a tune or chord progression. In many ways, it's more of a tool for composition or arranging than for improvisation, but even then, an understanding of reharmonization is a crucial skill for advanced improvisers. After all, if methods like these are used to derive new types of changes, you'll inevitably encounter situations in which you need to improvise over these changes.

Sometimes, the distinction between reharmonization and substitution is a bit hazy. How much can you alter a progression before it becomes a reharmonization? Substitutions can happen spontaneously on the part of the soloist and/or the rhythm section, while reharmonization is almost always premeditated—an obvious necessity in ensemble playing. Substitution tends not to disturb points of resolution within a song, while reharmonizations may obliterate some—sometimes all—of them, leaving the melody as the only point of reference.

Cycles

A *cycle* is a progression that moves in a consistent pattern. For example, the repeated I–VI–ii–V progression in the first part of the A section of Rhythm changes is a cycle; this root motion by descending 5th is cyclical, as is the the repetition of this four-chord unit.

On page 59 we looked at dominant cycles. In rehamonization, such cycles are often taken to a greater extreme. If the I chord in measure 5 of example 184 is used as the goal, a cycle can be set up to lead more dramatically to that goal, as in example 185, in the style of a progression used by Thelonious Monk in the A section of his early Rhythm changes tune "Humph."

Cycles can also be combined with other techniques such as tritone substitution and adding ii chords in front of *applied* (temporary) V chords. For example, look at this typical bridge from Rhythm changes.

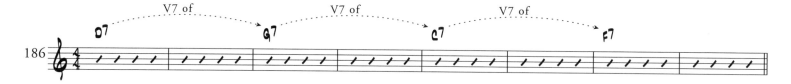

Now, check out this variation that Sonny Stitt used on "The Eternal Triangle."

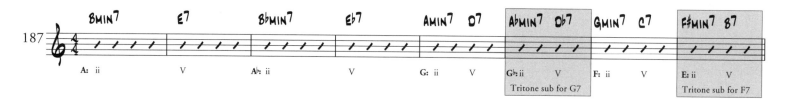

MATRICES AND "GIANT STEPS" CHANGES

A *harmonic matrix* is a tool used to create cycles that modulate through several keys in a set pattern. The idea of the matrix was introduced to jazz by John Coltrane in his groundbreaking tune "Giant Steps," though the use of matrices dates back to the bridge that Richard Rodgers wrote for the standard "Have You Met Miss Jones." A matrix is something from which something else originates.

The changes in example 188 are in the style of those 'Trane used in his landmark tune. They have become "standard" changes for advanced jazz musicians and have appeared verbatim in other tunes, such as Freddie Hubbard's "Dear John" and John McLaughlin's "Do You Hear the Voices."

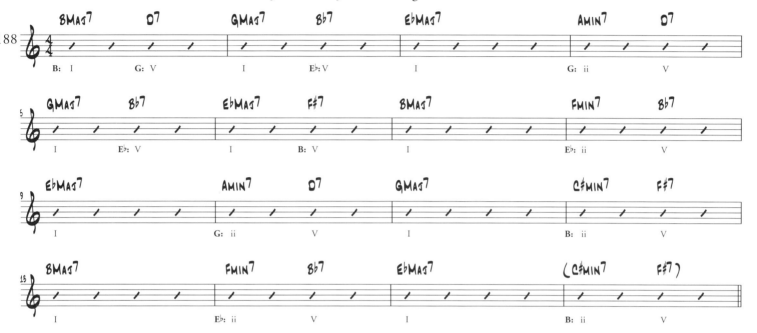

The changes in example 188 make use of an *augmented matrix*. The augmented triad containing the notes B, E♭ and G is used as the basis for the matrix. Each of these notes is used as a key center, and all of the chords in the progression lead to one of these key centers. Notice that augmented triads are symmetrical; that is, if you build an augmented triad using any note of that augmented triad as the root, you'll always get the same three pitches. For the sake of clarity, the same note spellings are used throughout.

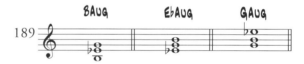

Other chords, especially symmetrical ones, can also be used as the basis for matrices. Example 190 shows a progression based on a *diminished matrix*; that is, it uses a diminished 7th chord as the basis for the key centers (in this case, B♭, D♭, E and G). This progression could also serve as a reharmonization for the first four bars of Rhythm changes.

These principles are often used by modern jazz musicians to reharmonize sections of standards (such as Coltrane's takes on "But Not For Me" and "Body and Soul"), for writing new tunes loosely based on existing tunes (like 'Trane's "26–2," and "Countdown," based on "Confirmation" and "Tune-Up," respectively), and for composing entirely new pieces with challenging harmonic structures that are still based on the practices of diatonic harmony.

OTHER CHORDS

In the lessons ahead, we'll be exploring some changes that are different from the diatonically based progressions we've looked at so far.

Certain types of chords that occur infrequently in bebop-based music are much more common in modern styles such as those we'll explore beginning on page 126. The two chords at right, for example, are both chords we've learned but haven't used much so far. In modern post-bebop compositions, however, they're used quite often.

Another type of chord that occurs more frequently in modern styles is the *bitonal triad* or *bichord*. A bitonal triad is any triad super-imposed over a bass note not found in that triad. These chords are used to great effect by modern composers like Keith Jarrett, Carla Bley and Steve Swallow. Bitonal triads often subtly imply certain 7th chords. For example, G♭/C implies C7alt.

Other chords, like those in example 193, are virtually never used in a diatonic bebop situation. At the same time, they illustrate the harmonic flexibility that's possible in modern styles.

There are often modal situations in modern tunes in which the momentary key center or scale, not a specific chord, is the focal point. In these situations, the trick is to be able to voice harmonies with flexibility within that scale. Example 194 shows the voicing associated with the Miles Davis's modal tune "So What" played throughout the D Dorian mode. The harmonies here are derived flexibly from within the mode; non of them are intended to function as an individual chord.

D Dorian—Diatonic "So What" Voicings

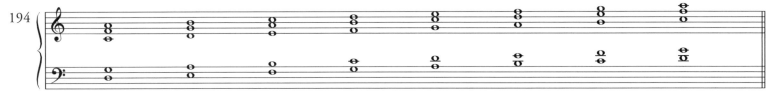

SIMPLE ELEMENTS FOR HIPNESS

Remember that this toolbox is meant to supplement the earlier toolboxes. There are certain tools among the more basic ones that will be particularly relevant to upcoming lessons. Sometimes in jazz, the "hippest" devices are actually fairly simple things that are taken out of their usual element and placed into a new context. It's therefore recommended that you take some time to review and practice the following tools, which will ensure that you have the necessary fluency to use them tools in the less predictable ways we'll be exploring.

- Chromatic Scale (page57)

- Intervals (page 11)

- Triads (page 13)

- Pentatonic Scales (page 10)

CONCEPTUAL CORNER:
DEVELOPING YOUR OWN STYLE

Finding the balance between individuality and conformity is a challenge we face in many facets of life. Likewise, no musician can escape being influenced by other musicians. Just the same, no good musician will allow him- or herself to be consumed by existing sounds so that individuality is completely lost. Most musicians end up somewhere between these two extremes, and the path to reaching this point is at the heart of developing one's own style.

Let's begin to explore developing a style by looking at some of the most influential tenor saxophonists in jazz. Listen to recordings by Coleman Hawkins, Lester Young, Dexter Gordon, Stan Getz, John Coltrane, Sonny Rollins, Warne Marsh, Joe Henderson and Wayne Shorter. No open-minded jazz fan or scholar would deny that each of these players swings mightily. Yet, closer examination reveals that each has a unique sense of swing. Phrasing, tone and melodic language also vary greatly from player to player in this all-star crowd, yet in each case these traits are compelling and well within the jazz idiom. Even jazz neophytes can emulate these jazz legends, in that we all can work to attain a personal sound that reflects our individuality while still fitting comfortably into the realm of jazz.

You've already begun to do this, whether you realize it or not. Unless you have equally enjoyed every note of jazz you've ever heard, you've already begun to categorize which sounds you like and which sounds you're less fond of. As you develop as a musican, these tastes will invariably change, which is part of the process. It's useful to analyze what specifically you do or don't like in a piece of music, but whether or not you do this, your feelings are bound to have an impact on your playing. The broader your scope of listening, the more organic your own sound is likely to be. If your life's ambition is to sound so much like Bill Evans that your playing is indistinguishable from his, this discussion isn't for you, but everyone else should consider that most music, whether or not it's your favorite, has something likeable in it. You may dislike a certain player's style, yet be very inspired by his or her playing on the first half-chorus of a solo on one tune from somebody else's album.

Remember that learning jazz is a process. If you find yourself going through an imitative period, join the club. Most, if not all, players go through stages in which their soloing sounds more derivative than original. This is perfectly natural, since at any moment you're improvising with whatever tools and language you have at your disposal. No one learns these things all at once, so if you haven't yet moved beyond your "Bud Powell" phase, don't fret. If, on the other hand, you've transcribed 20 Bud Powell solos without listening to anyone else, maybe it's time to move on and broaden your horizons.

If your tastes happen to be extreme—extremely avant-garde or extremely traditional—you need to weigh your personal vision against the potential for professional consequences. Let's say, for example, that you enjoy punctuating your solos by dropping your entire arm across the keyboard for a mega-cluster. By all means, you have the right to do that, but if the bandleader says, "Do that again and you're fired," you then have a choice to make. Certain styles are more sought after and more generally palatable than others, and this will vary over time and from place to place. If you don't quite fit in, you have several choices: Seek out an environment in which you do fit in; find a compromise that makes your playing more compatible with your environment; or, commit to following in the footsteps of others who have steadfastly maintained their individuality in spite of limited acceptance. Maybe acceptance will come, as it did for Thelonious Monk and Cecil Taylor; maybe it will be elusive, as it was for Herbie Nichols and Elmo Hope. Either way, you'll be true to your unique voice.

That said, many of us have broader tastes. Some of the most admired musicians are folks who can play in and adjust to any musical situation. Drummer Roy Haynes, reed players Yusef Lateef and Rahsaan Roland Kirk, bassists Ron Carter and Charles Mingus and vibraphonist Bobby Hutcherson are a few of the legendary musicians revered for their encyclopedic knowledge of their instruments' histories and their ability to fit into any sort of group or situation. In none of those cases are you likely to hear anybody criticize them for lacking a unique, individual sound. Among pianists, Mary Lou Williams, Billy Taylor, Dick Hyman, Jaki Byard and Marcus Roberts are especially admired for their ability to run the gamut of styles from stride to bop to modern, conservative to adventurous, all the while maintaining a sense of individuality.

CHAPTER 6 APPLICATIONS OF "DELUXE" TOOLS

SCALES, SCALES AND MORE SCALES

With the scales and modes we've learned to this point, the scale options for a given chord are tremendously broad. These charts summarize some of the many choices that are available. Depending on your sense of adventure, there are even more options, but the possibilities on the next few pages should keep you busy for a while. Assume that all scales begin on the same note as the root of the chord.

Scales for Major 7 Chords (including Maj6 and Maj7♯5 chords)

SCALE	NUMERIC FORMULA	CHORD COLORS IMPLIED
Major—(Ionian)	1, 2, 3, 4, 5, 6, 7, 1	9, 11(sus4), 13(6)
Major Pentatonic	1, 2, 3, 5, 6, 1	9, 13(6)
Lydian	1, 2, 3, ♯4, 5, 6, 7, 1	9, ♯11, 13
Lydian Augmented	1, 2, 3, ♯4, ♯5, 6, 7, 1	9, ♯11, ♯5, 13
Harmonic Minor: Mode 3	1, 2, 3, 4, ♯5, 6, 7, 1	9, 11(sus4), ♯5, 13
Harmonic Minor: Mode 6	1, ♯2, 3, ♯4, 5, 6, 7, 1	(♯9), ♯11, 13
Lydian Diminished: Mode 3	1, ♯2, 3, ♯4, ♯5, 6, 7, 1	(♯9), ♯11, ♯5, 13
Lydian Diminished: Mode 5 —(Harmonic Major)	1, 2, 3, 4, 5, ♭6, 7, 1	9, 11(sus4), ♭13(♯5)

Scales for Dominant 7 Chords

SCALE	NUMERIC FORMULA	CHORD COLORS IMPLIED
Mixolydian	1, 2, 3, 4, 5, 6, ♭7, 1	9, 11(sus4), 13
Major Pentatonic	1, 2, 3, 5, 6, 1	9, 13
Bebop (Dominant)	1, 2, 3, 4, 5, 6, ♭7, 7, 1	9, 11(sus4), 13
Blues (common version)	1, ♭3, 4, ♭5, 5, ♭7, 1	♯9, ♭5
Blues (alternate version)	1, ♭3, 3, 4, ♭5, 5, ♭7, 1	♯9, ♭5
Lydian ♭7	1, 2, 3, ♯4, 5, 6, ♭7, 1	9, ♯11, 13
Mixolydian ♭6	1, 2, 3, 4, 5, ♭6, ♭7, 1	9, 11(sus4), ♭13(♯5)
Altered	1, ♭2, ♭3, 3, ♭5, ♭6, ♭7, 1	♭9, ♯9, ♭5, ♯5
Half-Whole Diminished	1, ♭2, ♭3, 3, ♯4, 5, 6, ♭7, 1	♭9, ♯9, ♭5, 13
Whole-Tone	1, 2, 3, ♯4, ♯5, ♭7, 1	9, ♭5, ♯5
Harmonic Minor: Mode 5	1, ♭2, 3, 4, 5, ♭6, ♭7, 1	♭9, 11(sus4), ♭13,(♯5)
Lydian Diminished: Mode2	1, ♭2, 3, 4, 5, 6, ♭7, 1	♭9, 11(sus4), 13
Lydian Diminished: Mode 7	1, ♭2, ♭3, 3, 5, ♭6, ♭7, 1	♭9, ♯9, ♭13(♯5)

Scales for Minor 7 Chords

Scale	Numeric Formula	Chord Colors Implied
Natural Minor—(Aeolian)	1, 2, ♭3, 4, 5, ♭6, ♭7, 1	9, 11
Minor Pentatonic	1, ♭3, 4, 5, ♭7, 1	11
Blues	1, ♭3, 4, ♭5, 5, ♭7, 1	11
Dorian	1, 2, ♭3, 4, 5, 6, ♭7, 1	9, 11, 13(not on the ii)
Phrygian	1, ♭2, ♭3, 4, 5, ♭6, ♭7, 1	(♭9), 11
Bebop (Minor)	1, 2, ♭3, 4, 5, 6, ♭7, 7, 1	9, 11, 13(not on the ii)
Dorian ♭2	1, ♭2, ♭3, 4, 5, 6, ♭7, 1	(♭9), 11, 13(not on the ii)
Harmonic Minor: Mode 4	1, 2, ♭3, ♯4, 5, 6, ♭7, 1	9, (♯11), 13(not on the ii)

Additional Scales for "Tonic Minor" Chords (including min6 and min/Maj7 chords)

Scale	Numeric Formula	Chord Colors Implied
Minor Pentatonic (alternate version)	1, 2, ♭3, 5, 6, 1	6, 9, 11
Harmonic Minor	1, 2, ♭3, 4, 5, ♭6, 7, 1	7, 9, 11
Melodic Minor	1, 2, ♭3, 4, 5, 6, 7, 1	6, 7, 9, 11
*Whole-Tone	♭2, ♭3, 4, 5, 6, 7, ♭2	6, 7, (♭9), 11
Lydian Diminished	1, 2, ♭3, ♯4, 5, 6, 7, 1	6, 7, 9, (♯11)

*Beginning a half step away from the root

Scales for Minor 7♭5 Chords

Scale	Numeric Formula	Chord Colors Implied
Locrian	1, ♭2, ♭3, 4, ♭5, ♭6, ♭7, 1	(♭9), 11
Locrian ♯2	1, 2, ♭3, 4, ♭5, ♭6, ♭7, 1	9, 11, 13
Harmonic Minor: Mode 2	1, ♭2, ♭3, 4, ♭5, ♭6, ♭7, 1	(♭9), 11
Lydian Diminished: Mode 6	1, 2, ♭3, 4, ♭5, 6, ♭7, 1	9, 11

Scales for Diminished 7 Chords

Scale	Numeric Formula	Chord Colors Implied
Whole-Half Diminished	1, 2, ♭3, 4, ♭5, ♭6, 6, 7, 1	7, 9, 11, ♭13
Harmonic Minor: Mode 7	1, ♭2, ♭3, 3, ♭5, ♭6, 6, 1	♭13
Lydian Diminished	1, 2, ♭3, ♯4, 5, 6, 7, 1	7, 9,
Lydian Diminished: Mode 4	1, ♭2, ♭3, 4, ♭5, ♭6, 6, 1	11, ♭13

Example 195 is a one-chorus sample solo that uses most of the scales from from pages 100–101. It may seem like there are a lot of notes, but don't worry: This example should be played as a very slow ballad, using straight eighths. While not a realistic solo, the goal is to really dig in and hear how each of these scales works in context. The changes are in the style of those in "Body and Soul," one of the most played ballads in jazz history. That tune is perhaps most closely associated with Coleman Hawkins, and among its many other recordings are classics by Billie Holiday, John Coltrane, Benny Goodman and Dexter Gordon. The scales used are shown below the chord symbols. Note that the abbreviation "CTs" refers to chord tones.

CTs = Chord tones

Try using a variety of tunes to practice this application of many scales. Notice the effect that each scale has in a particular context. Does the scale create dissonance? Consonance? A little of both? How is it affected by emphasizing or de-emphasizing certain notes? How does its function change in different contexts? Your answers to questions like these will shape how you use the scales. Admittedly, in an actual performance of a ballad, it's unlikely that you'd cram that many notes and scales into a single chorus. Like any other new skill or concept, however, it's helpful to practice "to the extreme," so that in performance you have a broad palette of colors to use (or not use) in whatever way you wish.

Scales, Harmony and Gravity

Having experimented with these various scales, the next logical step is to examine the effects of their sounds. This is a particularly significant process when determining what to do with a dominant chord that is resolving. In his influential 1953 book, *The Lydian Chromatic Concept of Tonal Organization*, George Russell refers to this as "tonal gravity." In simplest terms, this means that some scales, usually those with more altered notes and thus more tension, create a stronger pull towards a point of resolution than others. Your scale choices on a dominant chord should therefore correspond with the intensity of tension and resolution you wish to create. This way of dealing with chord-scale relationships can be heard in the music of such artists as Bill Evans, David Baker, John Coltrane, Herbie Hancock and Jim Hall. The process becomes easier as you hone your theoretical and aural understanding of the different scales. Notice how much stronger the sense of tension and release is in example 196B than it is in example 196A.

As you get more fluent with this stuff, be aware that the effect of using a particular scale with a dominant chord depends more on the tonality towards which the chord is moving than on the relationship of the scale tones to the dominant chord itself. This is significant when substitution enters the picture. Example 197A uses the half-whole diminished scale. Example 197B uses the altered scale, which has even more dissonant colors and therefore a stronger pull. Example 197B also uses a tritone substitution, another dramatic device.

The truth of the matter is that example 197B creates a "double-negative" effect. While the altered scale has more altered color tones (four) in relation to a dominant chord than does the diminished scale (three), combining the altered scale with the tritone substitution negates much of the pull to the chord of resolution. None of the three altered notes in the diminished scale (D♭, A♭ and B♭) used in 197A coincides with notes in the key of resolution (C Major), while the altered scale used in 197B only contains one note (D♭) that creates tension against the key of resolution.

Another way to approach this idea of gravity is to use a combination of scales. This technique was central to the concept of *convergence* outlined by the great guitarist and educator Ted Dunbar in his 1975 book *A System of Tonal Convergence for Improvisors, Composers and Arrangers*. This concept is rather involved, but the essence revolves around a series of tones converging upon a point of resolution. Using a series of two or more scales that progress and intensify in their degree of tension can create a powerful convergence with an equally powerful resolution.

Example 199 shows the concept of convergence in action. The C7 lasts for a while before resolving to Fmin7, and the scales used over the C7 become more and more dissonant. This increases the buildup of tension as Fmin7 is approached, thereby increasing the resolution's intensity. Similar changes can be found in the A section of "Caravan," a tune written by Juan Tizol for Duke Ellington's band and also recorded brilliantly by Art Tatum, Ella Fitzgerald, Freddie Hubbard (both on his own and with Art Blakey) and Wynton Marsalis, among others.

Dubunking the Scale Myth

Warning: Don't read the following paragraph if you believe in Santa Claus, the Tooth Fairy or that Elvis Presley is still alive!

Still reading? Well, since you've proven that you can handle the emotional strain of having myths shattered, it's time for another one: Scales don't really exist. They are figments of the imagination, an arbitrary way of organizing sounds. All the same sounds that result from using scales would still exist if the perception of scales vanished tomorrow.

Does this mean that all of our scale study has been for nothing? Absolutely not. The fact is that words are imaginary too, but it would be rather difficult to communicate without them. Referring to scales is an excellent way of communicating ideas about certain sounds. Likewise, the way that notes are organized in scales provides a convenient and useful way to access these sounds, just as words can help us organize our thoughts, even when we are not speaking.

The point is this: As you advance in your jazz studies, you'll quite possibly find yourself moving beyond the need for scales. The more scales you learn, the more combinations of notes you'll have at your disposal. Then, when you solo, you may find that you're seeking certain notes that have the sound you want, not necessarily thinking of them as being part of a scale.

Let's say that you want to use the notes in example 200 over a C7 chord. You could say they're part of the C Altered scale or the C Half-Whole Diminished scale. You could also say they make up a scale you invented yourself, the "C Cucumber" scale. Better still, you could skip that whole part of the process and just use the notes. By all means, use scales and practice them thoroughly; just don't lose sight of the fact that scales are there so you can give yourself the greatest possible access to all the notes you could be using.

SIDE-SLIPPING

Many of the new scales we've been examining have some degree of *chromaticism* (the presence of notes that fall outside of the key or chord of the moment). We've actually been experimenting with the controlled use of chromaticism ever since we looked at the blues scale, through chromatic ornaments and altered notes on dominant chords. Now, we'll up the ante still further by examining the technique of *side-slipping* (sometimes referred to as *side-stepping*). Side-slipping involves temporarily leaving the tonality implied by the tune at that moment, then returning to it. The idea is rather similar to substitution: You add excitement to the harmony but ultimately return "home," rather than abandoning the core harmony altogether.

To get started with side-slipping, try choosing places in a tune where you want to leave the harmony (also choosing where you will return to it). In the places you've chosen, try moving a half step above or a half step below what you would normally play there, then find your way back. Take a look at the 32 bars in example 201. It's basically just a set of modes, those used for the landmark modal tunes "So What" and "Impressions." We will be using this "progression" in our discussion of side-slipping.

Side-slipping can be very useful when dealing with harmonies that are this static. Throwing in bop-style substitutions would not fit the style, but you may tire of playing nothing but the same seven notes for chorus after chorus. Side-slipping allows you to mix things up a bit—just make sure that you resolve convincingly, unless you're deliberately aiming for prolonged dissonance. Example 202 demonstrates this idea.

Modal tunes provide the most common context in which to use this technique. Not only do static harmonies create more need for variety, but faster-moving changes are more challenging to side-slip, since there is a lot less time to set the tonality, side-slip and return. Nonetheless, with practice this technique can be applied to standards and bop tunes. Trumpeter Woody Shaw was considered by many to be the master of this. One can hear this approach in renditions of standards by Shaw and other modernists like Dave Liebman, Steve Coleman and Pat Metheny. Here is an example of a rapid side-slip.

Note that when side-slipping, the left hand has two choices, just as in the case of more traditional substitution. The left hand may play the "normal" harmonies or can shift to harmonies more compatible with the notes used for side-slipping. The effects are very different but equally valid.

The changes in example 204 are in the style of Joe Henderson's modern classic "Inner Urge," a tune he recorded brilliantly in trio, quartet and big-band settings. Typically, the Lydian mode is used on all of the Maj7#11 chords, and this example is no exception. The one-chorus sample solo contains many instances in which the main tonality is side-slipped by a half step in either direction. These places are highlighted and labeled as to whether they side-slip "up" or "down," and to which harmony.

MELODIC INTERVALS REVISITED

In a sense, discussing intervals at this point in the game is sort of like discussing feet if you've already been walking for years: You've been using them all along, whether you think about them consciously or not. But, just as further examination of your feet can lead to new possibilities in hopping, skipping and dancing, further examination of certain intervals can lead to growth in your jazz vocabulary. Eddie Harris, Thelonious Monk, McCoy Tyner and Walter Bishop, Jr. are among the many jazz musicians who have experimented with soloing in a way that focuses on particular intervals.

Before we continue, it's important to make a distinction between two types of melodic intervals used in improvisation: *diatonic* intervals and *parallel* intervals. Diatonic intervals are those which change in quality depending on the chord or key of the moment. If using diatonic 3rds, for example, these 3rds would be either major or minor, depending on where you were in the scale or chord, while 4ths would be either perfect or augmented. Parallel intervals are those in which the exact interval remains constant throughout, so that in a passage of parallel major 3rds, all the 3rds would be major, while a passage of parallel perfect 4ths would contain only perfect (no augmented) 4ths. In such instances, the parallelism is maintained regardless of the key.

We've already spent a great deal of time using melodic 2nds and 3rds as tools for improvisation, even though you may not have thought of it in this way:

Diatonic 2nds: Virtually any scale passage that moves straight up or down consists of diatonic 2nds. Major scales, for example, consist entirely of major and minor 2nds.

Parallel 2nds: If you use parallel minor seconds, you get the chromatic scale. If you use parallel major 2nds, you get the whole-tone scale.

Diatonic 3rds: Virtually any arpeggio played straight up or down consists of diatonic 3rds. A min7♭5 arpeggio, for example, consists of a minor 3rd followed by two major 3rds.

Parallel 3rds: If you use parallel minor 3rds, you have the arpeggio of a diminished 7th chord. If you use parallel major 3rds, you have the arpeggio of an augmented triad.

What remains, then, is to examine melodic 4ths, 5ths, 6ths and 7ths. Fourths are, to put it one way, the most common among the less common intervals. The sound of 4ths is both recognizable and relevant, largely as a result of their prevalence in modern jazz voicings, in which context they were popularized by McCoy Tyner in the 1960s. Using 4ths in improvisation can be challenging, since 3rds are the basis of the chords used in most progressions used in jazz. When focusing on this interval, it's best to use parallel perfect 4ths wherever possible, adding augmented 4ths where a perfect 4th would be harmonically inappropriate. Melodically, 4ths can be played straight up or down in succession, as in example 205.

For both technical and musical reasons, however, this approach is not common. More typical is to play smaller groups of 4ths separated by stepwise motion or other intervals. Fourths are distinctive enough that the "4ths sound" is maintained even if other intervals are incorporated into a line; an occasional 2nd or 3rd will hardly destroy the effect.

Before exploring the improvisational options that larger intervals present, it's important to reinforce your awareness of *interval inversion*. As explained on page 93, an inversion is a reordering of the notes in an interval. Certain patterns emerge in interval inversion, and certain pairs of intervals are inversions of each other: 2nds and 7ths, 3rds and 6ths, and 4ths and 5ths. Major intervals become minor in inversion, while perfect intervals remain perfect. So, a major second inverts into a minor 7th, a minor 3rd inverts into a major 6th, and a perfect 4th inverts into a perfect 5th.

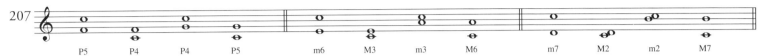

If you try soloing in 5ths, you may notice a similarity in sound with the sorts of lines you would play using 4ths. This is because your note choices will be very similar, the main difference being the subtly more spacious sound of 5ths.

When using 6ths and 7ths, the sheer width of the intervals can result in a very striking sound. These large spaces on the keyboard also present some technical challenges, since you cover a much wider distance with fewer notes. In most cases, the use of 6ths and 7ths means that you'll need to work out some technical kinks and to be creative in the way you connect the intervals.

Different intervals can also be helpful in practicing and mastering new scales. If you can play a scale up and down in the usual way—that is, in stepwise 2nds—why not try it in 3rds, 4ths and so on? Example 210 shows how you might apply this technique to the Lydian diminished scale (page 90).

The one-chorus sample solo in example 211 zeroes in on the use of 4ths. You'll find a few diatonic 4ths, but most of them are parallel. Note that the use of intervals as a soloing device can be particularly effective in combination with side-slipping, as happens in the final A section (beginning on measure 25). The changes are in the style of those in "Softly, as in a Morning Sunrise," a standard that has been recorded by such keyboard giants as Wynton Kelly, Sonny Clark, Martial Solal, Larry Young, Bobby Timmons, McCoy Tyner, Kenny Barron and Sir Roland Hanna.

The chorus in example 212 repeatedly shifts the focus to different diatonic and parallel intervals. Pay particular attention to the intervals used and the effects of each. These popular changes are in the style of those in the standard "Sweet Georgia Brown," which were also used in the 1950s by Thelonious Monk ("Bright Mississippi"), Jackie McLean ("Donna," aka "Dig") and Clifford Brown ("Sweet Clifford"). The first 16 bars are also are used for the bridge of "Caravan," whose A section was alluded to on page 105.

Pentatonic Scales Revisited

Superimposition

Practically all of the scales we've looked at so far have been used in a context in which they're built on the same note as the chord(s) they're played over. Now, we'll begin to look at how to *superimpose* scales—that is, how to take a scale out of its usual context and use it elsewhere. In a sense, we've already done just that through the use of modes. However, the most common application of scale superimposition involves the use of pentatonic scales, which we looked at on page 10.

You can superimpose the major pentatonic scale (or minor pentatonic, which is itself a mode of the major pentatonic) over various chords in various ways by beginning the scale on notes other than the root of the chord. The sound of a scale superimposed in this way is very modern and colorful, yet the earthy nature of pentatonic scales makes the sound more accessible. The use of superimposed pentatonics became popular in the 1960s, largely through the playing of keyboard greats like Chick Corea, McCoy Tyner, Herbie Hancock, Bill Evans, Steve Kuhn, Joe Zawinul and Larry Young.

The concept of superimposition is pretty simple. Begin with a pentatonic scale in which the notes are compatible with the chord, and play the scale over that chord. It's common, for example, to use a major pentatonic scale beginning beginning a whole step (or major 2nd, or 9th) above the root of a Maj7 chord.

People often describe the sound of pentatonic scales as "open," since the five notes create a sense of space compared to seven-note scales. On modal tunes, pentatonics are useful when that sort of openness is desired. On tunes with more changes, superimposed pentatonics create a sound that is both open and modern, and yet is still compatible with the changes.

The chart below shows some of the most common pentatonic superimpositions. The first and third columns show where to begin the major pentatonic scale in relation to the root of the chord; the second and fourth columns show the chord colors that result from using that scale. For example, the chart shows that you can begin a major pentatonic scale on the 2 above the root of any Maj7 chord, and it will imply the colors 9, 3, ♯11, 13 and 7.

Major Pentatonic Superimpositions

Maj7 and 6	Chord Colors Implied	min7, min6, & min/Maj7	Chord Colors Implied
1	1, 9, 3, 5, 13(6)	♭3	♭3, 11, 5, ♭7, 1
2	9, 3, ♯11, 13, 7	4	11, 5, 6, 1, 9
5	5, 13, 7, 9, 3	♭6	♭13, ♭7, 1, ♭3, 11
Dominant 7	**Chord Colors Implied**	♭7	♭7, 1, 9, 11, 5
1	1, 9, 3, 5, 13	**min7♭5**	**Chord Colors Implied**
2	9, 3, ♯11, 13, 7*	♭5	♭5, ♭13, ♭7, ♭9, ♭3
♭3	♯9, 4(11)*, 5, ♭7, 1	**dim7**	**Chord Colors Implied**
4 ("sus" sound)	4, 5, 13, 1, 9	2	2, 3*, ♭5, 6, 7
♭5	♭5, ♯5, ♭7, ♭9, ♯9	4	11, 5*, 6, 1, 9
♯5	♯5, ♭7, 1, ♯9, 4(11)*	♭6	♭13, ♭7*, 1, ♭3, 11
6	13, 7*, ♭9, 3, ♭5	7	7, ♭9*, ♭3, ♭5, ♭13
♭7 ("sus" sound)	♭7, 1, 9, 4, 5		

*This note will likely clash with the notes in the chord, and should therefore be used with caution. Such notes need not be avoided entirely; just be aware that they should be de-emphasized unless a deliberately dissonant effect is desired.

The one-chorus solo in example 214 is constructed entirely from major pentatonic scales. Notice both the overall sound and the sound of each different superimposition. The changes are in the style of those in the standard "On Green Dolphin Street," which has been recorded by the likes of Miles Davis, Eric Dolphy, Bill Evans, Chet Baker and Tito Puente.

Combining Pentatonic Scales

Once you have some fluency with superimposing pentatonic scales, you can take the next step and combine them, which creates a very colorful effect that's somewhat different from the effect created by combining scales as we did on pages 104-105. The rationale for combining pentatonic scales is similar to that for side-slipping: A single pentatonic scale, containing only five notes, may start to feel stifling after a while. By having the option of switching to different pentatonic scales, you increase the variety in your note choices while retaining the earthy, open sound that would lead you to choose a pentatonic scale in the first place.

As with side-slipping, combining pentatonic scales works best with modal tunes or other tunes with slow-moving changes. Note that most standards don't stay on any one chord long enough to make the use of multiple pentatonic scales necessary (or possible).

Using Outside Pentatonic Scales

Another option is the use of *outside* pentatonic scales, pentatonic scales that wouldn't generally be thought of as compatible with the harmony. In jazz, "outside" (or just "out") most often implies dissonance—literally, outside of the standard harmonies or note choices.* In the 1960s, John Coltrane and McCoy Tyner made significant and influential use of outside pentatonics. While "outness" can be taken to even greater extremes (see page 132), this application is tamed somewhat by, once again, the earthy accessibility of the pentatonic sound. Using roughly the same guidelines as in side-slipping (that is, you can move to a different tonality if you "bring it back" at a well-calculated moment), you can choose outside pentatonic scales to create more tension and variety. How and where you choose to release the tension and return to "normal" harmony is up to you. A technique popularized by Tyner is to play a low-register open 5th (that is, the root and 5th of a chord) with your left hand (unless you're playing the bass line) to more firmly establish the tonality when you return.

* Note that in conversation, jazz musicians also use "out" to denote anything that is strange, whether music-related or not:

"Man, that cat is so out. I asked him his name and he just laughed and squeezed my nose."
"I was playing a solo and the outest thing happened—the ceiling caved in!"
"I was hanging with Fred and he started takin' it out, talking about aliens, so I had to split."

Example 217 is a sample chorus that uses multiple pentatonic superimpositions. This example is based on the "So What/Impressions"–style harmonies we looked at on page 106, probably the most common modal progression in all of modern jazz. Notice that the second and last A sections use outside pentatonics, and that in each case, resolution is achieved by the end of the section.

TRIADS REVISITED

Even more basic and earthy than the major pentatonic scale is the humble triad. If you've studied more advanced voicing concepts, you've probably encountered *superimposed* or *upper-structure triads*—a "color" triad sounded over a 7th chord. As long as the added colors are compatible with the underlying harmony, superimposed triads can be an effective soloing tool. The effect is similar to that of superimposed pentatonics: The colors create a sound that is modern and hip, yet the familiar sound of the triad makes it accessible. Example 218 shows the added colors that result from superimposing different triads over a CMaj7 chord. You're encouraged to experiment with triads relating to all types of 7th chords.

Example 219 demonstrates the use of triads in an improvisation over bebop-style changes. (Triads implied by the melody, as opposed to those that make up the underlying harmony, are shown in gray.) The changes are in the style of Tadd Dameron's classic "Lady Bird," a tune recorded by such keyboard artists as Bud Powell, Mel Rhyne, Mary Lou Williams, Harold Mabern, Sun Ra, Barry Harris, Horace Parlan Andy LaVerne and Tete Montoliu. Other notable recordings of "Lady Bird" include those by Charles Mingus, Art Blakey, Fats Navarro, Red Rodney, Stan Getz, Dizzy Gillespie and Miles Davis (who also recycled the changes for his own "Half Nelson").

Note that outside triads are a good option when more tension is desired. Earlier discussions of side-slipping (page 106) and outside pentatonics (page 112) should provide you with a good conceptual basis for getting your feet wet with this application of triads. Even the most outside triads, to perhaps an even greater extent than is true of pentatonics, have a surprising capacity to sound like they belong.

CONCEPTUAL CORNER:
SINGING WHILE PLAYING

We keyboard players have all the luck. All of the information we need is displayed visually on the keyboard. We can use the sustain pedal to create lush washes of sound. We can play chords. We can even play chords with one hand while the other hand does something else. There is, however, one thing that we're not able to do: make the instrument really sing. On the organ, we have a greater ability to sustain notes, while on the piano we have a greater ability to control dynamics. In neither case, however, can we produce the voice-like inflections of a trumpet or saxophone, nore can we bend and smear notes in the way that a trombonist or guitarist can. Still, there are things we can do to bring out whatever lyricism and singing quality we can. Singing while playing is one way—and a fabulous one—to do this.

In this case, what we mean by "singing while playing" is singing along with a solo line as we play it (crooning "The Wind Beneath My Wings" while plunking out chords is also singing while playing, but that's a topic for another book). Probably the most admired proponent of this technique is not a pianist at all, but rather a guitarist: George Benson. Benson has also had a noteworthy career as a vocalist, and his singing adds a very enjoyable flavor to the sound of his guitar solos. Among pianists, the most famous proponent of this technique is Keith Jarrett. Jarrett, however, is not known as a vocalist, and in fact has endured a great deal of criticism for his singing. In this discussion, we look to Jarrett for inspiration.

So, why is it Jarrett, and not Benson, that we should seek to emulate? In Benson's case, singing adds texture to his solos, something that's worth trying if your singing voice is as nice as his. In Jarrett's case, on the other hand, singing is ultimately incidental to the overall sound—that is, his singing is simply a reflection of his connection with the touch and sound of the piano. It is as though he is trying to sing through his fingers in order to overcome the piano's non-vocal (even anti-vocal) nature, and his touch and sound prove that it is far from a lost cause. The primary goal of singing while playing is not to match each pitch exactly with your voice, but to use singing as a means of expression and spontaneity. Keith Jarrett is far from the only keyboard great to engage in this practice; on many recordings, including some by the likes of Art Tatum and Bud Powell, you'll hear singing or grunting in the background of the piano solos.

Does this mean that you need to sing along with your solos in order to play expressively? Of course not. Does it mean that when you perform you should grunt at the top of your lungs, even when playing softly, showing no regard for how it impacts the overall sound? Of course not. Think of it in this way: Keyboards are cold, mechanical machines. Even the piano, with all its resonance of tone and capacity for dynamics and sensitivity, is a cold, mechanical machine if you depress a key with no feeling. It is the human element that transforms these machines into expressive artistic tools. Obviously, you must have control over certain technical elements—correct finger placement, posture, dexterity, etc.—but none of these set a piano apart from a socket wrench, computer keyboard, steering wheel or lawnmower. Now, think for a moment about singing a song—maybe "Happy Birthday" at a party or your favorite song in the shower. It may or may not sound good, but it's still an entirely visceral experience. Singing while playing a solo line at the piano can help make it a less mechanical experience and help you to tap into the same kind of *feeling*. You may or may not choose to sing in this way when you perform, but using it as a practice tool is likely to help your expressivity, probably in ways that will carry over even when you're not singing along.

Singing can be helpful in other ways as well. In our look at transcription on pages 39–41, we explored singing as a tool for digging into the contours of a recorded solo. The contours that you like best are likely to stick and find expression as you solo. The voice can be especially effective as the impetus or inspiration for a phrase, since keyboardists always run the risk of favoring phrases that fit nicely under the hand, even if they aren't necessarily musically expressive. Singing can also be helpful in preventing phrases from getting too long. One of the things that give logic and shape to a solo line is the silence between phrases, one of the elements that helps music breathe. Yet, while that breathing is physically necessary for a vocalist or horn player, the nature of the keyboard allows for lines that can go on indefinitely. Singing forces you to limit your phrase length in a way that creates a natural, organic musical flow. Remember that that one meaning of "inspiration" is the taking in of breath.

Soloing On Coltrane Changes

For many aspiring jazz musicians, the prospect of soloing over *Coltrane changes* (such as those for "Giant Steps") is intimidating, but there's really no cause for anxiety. This is not to say that these changes are easy or can be played successfully without practice. However, what they have going for them is that they are based entirely on the principles of harmony that we've studied extensively in other, "simpler" jazz repertoire. The challenge lies in the speed at which modulation occurs, and the goal therefore becomes one of dexterity—being able to adjust to each chord and modulation with little time to prepare. It is for this reason that patterns are a popular method for getting through these changes. Example 220 uses such a pattern over a Coltrane-type progression.

In order to remain within a manageable range when using patterns such as this, it's sometimes more practical to find a pattern that combines upward and downward motion; otherwise, you may quickly run out of keys.

Ultimately, there's a limit to the utility of patterns such as these, unless you're using them as a practice device to help you woodshed the changes. In theory, you should have no less flexibility or creativity with Coltrane changes than with any others; it will just take more practice to get there. The sample solo in example 222 uses one chorus of changes in the style of "Giant Steps," with which you can use the same devices and techniques we looked in Chapter 4.

Once you've reached a comfort level with Coltrane-type changes, you can take things a step further. If your chops are up to it—and all that takes is practice—you can apply more sophisticated devices to changes with matrices, which we looked at on page 97. Various scales, superimposed pentatonics and triads and other advanced techniques are all at your disposal. Just be aware that the distinctive sound of some scales may not come through on certain fast-moving changes, since you won't always have time to use enough of a scale's most characteristic notes.

The changes in example 223 are in the style of those Coltrane used in his remarkable, change-shredding vehicle "Countdown," itself a superimposition of augmented matrices (marked with black brackets) onto the changes from "Tune Up." The "Countdown" changes have become a standard workout for advanced jazz musicians. Among the jazz musicians that recorded "Countdown" in the 1980s and '90s are Anthony Braxton, Brad Mehldau, Steve Kuhn, Billy Harper, Kenny Garrett and Benny Green.

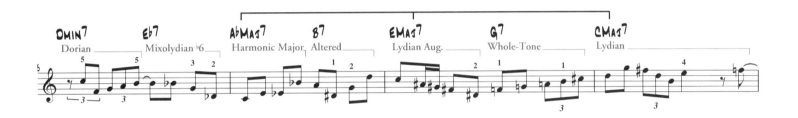

MULTI-NOTE SOLO DEVICES: BLOCK CHORDS AND MORE

As we add to our list of intensity-building techniques, it's worth taking a look at some of the options that exist beyond different ways of playing single-note lines, since, the ability to play multiple notes is one of the special capabilities of keyboard instruments. Each of the techniques discussed on pages 120 and 121 will be shown over a 12-bar blues in F.

The spiky, startling character of clusters, which we briefly looked at on page 93, makes for a good high-energy device, though clusters can be also be used in a delicate, subtle manner. Clusters can be immensely useful in avant-garde or free playing, but they can also be put to use in a straight-ahead context by choosing notes that are compatible with the changes, as in example 224.

The transition from single notes to locked-hands style block chords is another effective way to bring the energy level up a notch. Example 225 applies the locked-hands technique that we explored on page 94 using close-position chords. Remember that the left hand plays the bottom note in each voicing. Organists using their left hands for bass lines can still use these harmonies by simply omitting the bottom note in each chord.

On page 60, we looked at the use of parallel octaves in the right hand, a device often associated with the blues and soul jazz, largely through its association with the great pianist Bobby Timmons. Parallel octaves can be a very effective high-energy device. By combining the octaves with identical left-hand rhythms (with any voicings you choose), you can create another kind of block chord, as in example 226.

Another octave-related dramatic device octaves is two-handed unison lines played two octaves apart, as demonstrated in example 227. This technique is closely associated with Phineas Newborn, Jr., though others have used it as well. Note that because neither hand plays chords, you'll either need to be satisfied with harmonic ambiguity or ensure that the lines make the changes with particular clarity. The use of two-handed unisons is primarily a piano technique, and it requires significant left-hand woodshedding for effective use.

CONCEPTUAL CORNER:
OUTSIDE THE $\frac{4}{4}$ BOX—OTHER TIME SIGNATURES

One of the ways you can achieve variety from tune to tune is by playing tunes with time signatures other than $\frac{4}{4}$. Although there were a handful of non-$\frac{4}{4}$ tunes in jazz before the 1950s (notably Benny Carter's "Waltzing the Blues" and Fats Waller's "Jitterbug Waltz"), such examples were rare, and the consensus was that one could only swing in $\frac{4}{4}$. Several musicians in the 1950s began to change that. Dave Brubeck's album *Time Out* introduced many people to less common time signatures, thanks largely to "Take Five," Paul Desmond's classic tune in $\frac{5}{4}$. Around the same time, drummer Max Roach made several recordings of jazz waltzes that proved that other time signatures could really swing, while Miles Davis included the classic jazz waltz "All Blues" on his 1959 album *Kind Of Blue*. Waltzes have since become common in jazz, and later generations of musicians have learned to swing naturally in $\frac{3}{4}$. At the same time, many musicians have taken on music in $\frac{5}{4}$, $\frac{7}{4}$, and other *odd* or *asymmetrical* time signatures as a new challenge and source of stimulation. Modern-day jazz musicians often take songs in $\frac{4}{4}$ and rearrange them for other time signatures. As with other aspects of jazz, the creative use of different time signatures is an example of jazz musicians' creative restlessness and spirit of innovation.

$\frac{3}{4}$ or Waltz Time

Many early examples of jazz waltzes now sound a bit stiff—not surprising, since all big developments in jazz had to that point made use of $\frac{4}{4}$ time. By the 1960s, however, musicians were becoming comfortable with waltzes, as evidenced by recordings of standard waltzes like "My Favorite Things" (John Coltrane) and "Someday my Prince Will Come" (Miles Davis), as well as of other modern standards in three, including "Bluesette" (Toots Thielemans), "A Child Is Born" (Thad Jones), "Waltz for Debby" (Bill Evans), "Little Niles" (Randy Weston), "Up Jumped Spring" (Freddie Hubbard) and "West Coast Blues" (Wes Montgomery). As others began to innovate with music that was less symmetrical than music of the bop tradition, waltzes proved to be a great vehicle for such innovations. Wayne Shorter, for example, included a brilliant modern waltz—for example, "Wildflower," "Night Dreamer," "Footprints" and "Miyako"—on each of several albums.

How to approach a waltz depends on the style in which it occurs. Because there are three beats to the measure, the usual backbeat is obviously impossible, so the swing-eighth feeling is of vital importance and must be played with conviction.

When playing standards and standard-like tunes, your approach can be virtually identical to the way you would play in $\frac{4}{4}$. On more modern tunes, you usually have more rhythmic flexibility, which requires in turn that you be comfortable enough with the beat that you don't need to state it explicitly at all times.

$\frac{5}{4}$, $\frac{7}{4}$ and Other Time Signatures

If you listen to a tune like "Take Five," you'll notice that it relies on insistent *vamps* (short, repeated passages, usually comprised of only a few chords). While the vamping sounds great, it also ensures that the players and listeners don't lose the beat. Many players of later generations have internalized the "trickier" time signatures as naturally as $\frac{4}{4}$ or $\frac{3}{4}$, which has allowed them to become rhythmically unfettered. There's no great secret to attaining this level of facility, aside from choosing to make a priority of practicing playing in $\frac{5}{4}$, $\frac{7}{4}$ and so on. One helpful tool is to divide measures into smaller units. For example, the $\frac{5}{4}$ vamp in "Take Five" can naturally be divided into a measure of $\frac{3}{4}$ and a measure of $\frac{2}{4}$. Likewise, many tunes in seven can be divided into four plus three, three plus four, etc. Just be careful that such subdivisions follow the natural flow of the music.

Modern composers like Charles Mingus and Joanne Brackeen have made use of several time signatures within a single tune. Others, like Ornette Coleman, have written music that indicates the number of beats in a measure, but which contains no bar lines. Music in this vein requires two things before you can really dig in: First, you need to be comfortable enough with each of the signatures within a tune that switching between them is effortless; second, you should try to be familiar with that composer's sound. Composers often use changes of time signature to achieve a certain sound that makes intuitive sense, even when intellectually challenging.

Hemiola

Most of the techniques we've studied so far in this chapter are ways of controlling intensity and variety through note choices. Over pages 123–125, we'll shift the focus to using rhythm as a tool for controlling intensity and variety.

We've already examined the process of superimposition in the context of pentatonic scales and triads. *Hemiola* is a kind of rhythmic superimposition. Hemiola, also referred to as *polyrhythm*, is the act of superimposing one time signature over another. In the context of improvisation, this involves playing passages that imply a meter that contrasts with the written or "expected" meter of the tune. One way to do this is to simply imagine the superimposed meter in your mind's ear as you play. This "imagining" will often lead to phrasing and accents that naturally bring out the polyrhythm. Example 228, while written in $\frac{4}{4}$, actually sounds as though written in three.

This technique is much more effective if the left-hand comping (example 229A) or bass lines (example 229B) also reflect the polyrhythm.

Another effective technique for bringing out a polyrhythm is the use of patterns. The ear naturally latches on to the repetition of a pattern, which can help to clearly delineate polyrhythms. By the same token, the potential monotony of repeating a pattern is greatly tempered in a hipper rhythmic or harmonic context (as opposed to playing, for example, a Hanon exercise over ii–V–I). Example 230 shows the use of a pattern in $\frac{4}{4}$ that creates the aural illusion of $\frac{5}{8}$.

Inspired in large part by the Miles Davis rhythm section of the 1960s (which included Herbie Hancock, Ron Carter and Tony Williams), some advanced modern rhythm sections will uniformly adopt a polyrhythm in performance. In other words, the whole rhythm section may work with the polyrhythm until the entire groove has shifted to one that relates to the superimposed rhythm. Ideally, this occurs only in cases in which the players have the rhythmic fluency to get smoothly and accurately back to the original meter and groove.

RHYTHMIC DISPLACEMENT

Rhythmic displacement is the act of shifting a line rhythmically. In other words, an entire line is moved forward or backward by a certain number of beats, so that beats, accents and changes occur away from their expected locations. This is also referred to as *playing over the bar lines*, since one of the fundamental functions of barlines—outlining the placement of beats—is significantly altered. Lennie Tristano, Bill Evans, Paul Bley and Keith Jarrett are among the most influential practitioners of this technique, and it can be heard in the playing of many other keyboard artists who followed them including Geri Allen, Kenny Kirkland and Brad Mehldau. The big challenge is being able to keep track of the tune's core structure, yet feeling free enough for the displaced lines to flow.

One way to practice and use rhythmic displacement is to take an ordinary line that you might use in a normal context and shift the entire line forward or backward by a fixed number of beats. Try playing the passage in example 231.

Now, shift the entire line backward by an eighth note (that is, play the first sounding note on the downbeat), as in example 232. This is another instance in which a distinctive, well-constructed line can help the ear forgive the new, much different, rhythmic feeling.

Then try shifting the line forward (from the original) by two full beats.

You can also approach displacement with more flexibility about the changes and where they fall rhythmically. In example 234, the normal changes are shown above the staff, the shifted ones below; notice the different effects of each. As you decide on such displacement of the changes, build your lines accordingly.

Even if you're not interested in using rhythmic displacement in your own soloing, there are compelling reasons to become comfortable with it. Most significant is the possibility that you'll be playing with others who use it themselves. Some influential modern drummers, such as Jack DeJohnette and Jeff "Tain" Watts, have helped popularize the use of rhythmic displacement, and it has become increasingly common among drummers in that style. As a result, there can be a sort of tightrope act that you should be prepared for if you're going to play with such drummers. If you hear a drummer playing a half beat away from where he or she "should" be playing, is it an accident that you should instantly compensate for, or is it on purpose? If the latter, your goal becomes to correctly orient your playing to that of the drummer, all the while keeping track of the original beat to which you'll both eventually return.

Example 235 is a one-chorus solo that uses both hemiola and displacement. Watch for where and how these devices are used. If there is a polyrhythm, what feeling does it create? If displacement occurs, where do the displaced chords land? Notice that in some cases, the two devices are combined, as the use of polyrhythms often leads to an implied shift or displacement of the bar lines. The changes and form are in the style of the classic "Someday My Prince Will Come," popularized in a jazz context by Miles Davis. This tune has since been recorded by a diverse group of keyboard artists, including Bill Evans, Oscar Peterson, Wynton Kelly, Dave Brubeck, Dorothy Donnegan, Alan Broadbent, Fred Hersch, Kenny Werner, Dr. Lonnie Smith, Michel Petrucciani and Renee Rosnes. The entrances of the displaced harmonies are shown in gray.

PLAYING ON NON-DIATONIC CHANGES

In the 1960s, some composers and players began to experiment extensively with *non-diatonic harmony*—chord progressions that are difficult or impossible to define through the theory and vocabulary of traditional harmony. The idea wasn't completely new; musicians such as Thelonious Monk and Charles Mingus had used such techniques before, usually in sections of tunes that were largely diatonic. However, it is the Miles Davis Quintet of the 1960s that is credited with establishing this sound in the jazz vocabulary. Each of the four sidemen in this group—Herbie Hancock, Wayne Shorter, Ron Carter and Tony Williams—contributed original compositions in this vein. Through their playing of these and other tunes, they explored and developed the possibilities of playing within a looser, less traditional harmonic structure. Among the other giants of that era who contributed great non-diatonic tunes to the jazz legacy are trumpeters Woody Shaw and Booker Little, saxophonists Eric Dolphy, Jackie McLean and Joe Henderson, pianists Andrew Hill and Chick Corea, vibraphonist Bobby Hutcherson and drummer Joe Chambers. Many composers whose music is considered more mainstream, such as Cedar Walton, Kenny Dorham, Benny Golson, Gil Evans and Freddie Hubbard, borrowed significantly from this concept of increased harmonic flexibility.

Now, let's move on from history to practice. We've already looked at some modal tunes that don't follow diatonic structures, and we've also touched on some changes that don't behave "normally," such as the last eight measures of example 204 on page 107. Further, we've looked at ways of playing based on a chord-scale relationship rather than focusing on traditional change-making methods. So, what happens when we encounter a progression like the one in example 236?

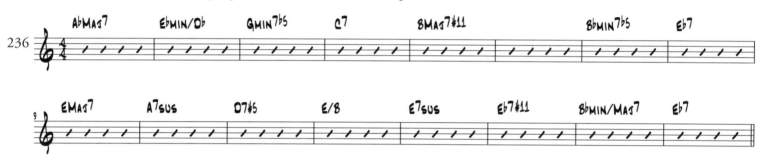

These changes are like those used by Wayne Shorter on his "Nefertiti." On the original recording of that tune (with Miles Davis), the only real soloist is the drummer, though others have since recorded the tune with solos, including piano-led versions by Chick Corea, Kenny Drew, Jr., Kei Akagi and Richie Beirach. There are a couple of fleeting moments, such as measures 3–5, when it could be said that the harmony is diatonic. For the most part, however, the harmonic colors fall well outside of the norms we've studied. From a certain standpoint, making the changes is making the changes and you should be able to use the usual techniques in such cases, as in example 237 (based on the last eight measures of example 236).

However, bebop-based methods of choosing notes are not entirely compatible with changes such as these. These kinds of changes are different and beg to be played differently, as we'll find on page 127.

Getting from chord to chord is still an issue, even with the kinds of changes we looked at in examples 236 and 237. Where soloing on bebop and standard changes entails bringing out the sound of chord tones, soloing on non-diatonic changes quite often involves bringing out the "color tones." The 9ths, 11ths, 13ths and altered notes on certain dominant chords are essential to the richness of these kinds of harmonies, and it's important to focus on these notes when soloing. The resulting sound is much more open than the change-shredding of a bebop line. As for which notes to use to fill in the gaps, we now have a wide array of scales to choose from. You should be able to find a scale for any chord, including chords you've never played before. Even passages straight from the chromatic scale are possible, since on this sort of harmony there is less pressure to be inside the changes. On the two-chorus sample solo in example 238, pay attention to the way in which color tones are emphasized.

Having spent some time examining the issue of note choice, let's look at some of the intangibles that can make the difference between a competent solo over non-diatonic changes and a thoroughly convincing one. When you listen to a great modern artist such as Herbie Hancock, Keith Jarrett, Chick Corea or Larry Young playing a tune in this non-diatonic style, you'll find that their note choices are indeed "noteworthy." At the same time, the notes—that is, the pitches—only tell a small part of the story. Herbie's rhythm, phrasing and lyricism are what make his solos exceptional.

One of the benefits of playing this sort of tune is that you're not encumbered by the constant need to make the changes. Assuming you have sufficient vocabulary to deal with chords, you can focus on more basic things like melody and rhythm. By the same token, if you neglect these basic elements, you don't have the constant churn of ii–V–Is to keep things interesting. This is the kind of situation in which you'll be glad to have developed a firm grasp of basic melody-making principles like good swing feel, contour, rhythmic variety, pacing, tension and release and so on. If you feel stuck, go back and review the basic principles and work to apply them to these kinds of advanced situations. More advanced melodic concepts such as polyrhythms, side-slipping and the use of multiple scales can also be quite relevant.

One of the most effective ways to focus on the basic elements is to pay attention to melodic development. If you pull every note out of thin air, it's hard to come up with a cohesive solo. However, if you work to develop your stream of consciousness in a way that encourages a logical progression of ideas, a single phrase may create its own momentum.

If, for example, you begin with this phrase…

…you can use a transformed version of it for the next phrase…

…followed by even more transformation.

Having built up a great deal of intensity through the reworking of the original phrase, it might be a good time to release some tension by playing a contrasting phrase.

By no means is it necessary for you to follow this sort of process exactly. This is just an example of how the use of melodic development can not only stimulate ideas and content for your solo, but also make them cohere into a logical, compelling statement—rather than sounding like just a bunch of notes.

The sample solo in example 243 uses one chorus of changes in the style of Herbie Hancock's popular tune "Dolphin Dance." Definitive versions of this tune have been recorded by Hancock, Bill Evans and Ahmad Jamal, along with lesser-known versions by Charles Earland, Claude Williamson, Mike Nock, Uri Caine and Michele Rosewoman. Pay attention to the melodic development, and note the harmonic contrast between change-making phrases and more color-oriented passages. Like many tunes and progressions in this style, these changes run the gamut from clearly diatonic progressions (measures 4–5) to chords whose functions are more difficult to define (measures 32–33).

PLAYING "COLORS" ON A STANDARD

At this point, it's important to understand that the non-diatonic approach we've just been exploring isn't relevant only to non-diatonic tunes. Of course, you can certainly choose to stick with the traditional change-making routine on a tune composed of ii–Vs, and some situations particularly warrant that approach. It may be, for example, that you're playing a lot of Wayne Shorter tunes in a set and need some beboppers thrown in for variety. Or, it may be that you simply prefer bebop to more modern stuff. In any event, you should be aware that you can also apply a more color-oriented* approach to playing standards.

Let's take Rhythm changes as an example. The A section is packed with changes, which usually inspires the approach of outlining the chords in the clearest way possible.

However, there's no law that prohibits taking a different approach. Using the techniques we've looked at for playing colors, we can instead focus more on thematic development and other melody-building ideas. As for note choices, we can pick tones that are more colorful, but which still relate to the harmony. The result will likely be an open-sounding line that is harmonically ambiguous, yet doesn't clash with the Rhythm changes.

Here are some possibilities for incorporating colors into a solo over standard (that is, mainly diatonic) changes:

- Begin with colors and build toward change-making.

- Begin with change-making and build toward colors.

- Use colors in the middle of a solo, "bookending" it with a change-making approach.

- Incorporate colors intermittently throughout the solo.

- Pass up traditional change-making entirely, and play colors for an entire solo.

Ultimately, there are two significant reasons to make the changes from a bebop approach on any tune. First: You like the sound. Second: You're trying to show listeners and fellow musicians your change-making prowess. For some, those reasons are compelling enough to play nothing but bebop for an entire career. For others, neither of these reasons has real significance. Your own choices in how to approach a tune will depend on your own feelings. If you find that you're playing a lot of standards and are consistently bored by traditional change-making, it may be worth seeking out more compatible repertoire.

* Keep in mind that here, "colors" refers to a certain approach to dealing with harmony. Obviously, you'll be making use of colors whether or not that is your primary goal.

Example 246 is a sample solo chorus with changes in the style of "You and the Night and the Music," a popular standard among pianists and recorded by the likes of Bill Evans, Dave McKenna, George Shearing, Hampton Hawes, Keith Jarrett, Marian McPartland, Mulgrew Miller, Mark Levine, Kevin Hays and Hector Martignon. The solo is mostly in the kind of color-oriented style that you might use on a non-diatonic modern tune—where non-diatonic devices are applied to a standard. Notice the way in which the final A section returns to more of a change-making approach, providing contrast and a release from the harmonically floating feeling of the first 24 measures.

FREEDOM

Free jazz is a nebulous term that means different things to different people (live bebop with no cover charge doesn't count). Typically, it refers to adventurous and often dissonant jazz in which the musicians free themselves from some of the structures—chord changes, time signatures, repetitive forms and so on—central to straight-ahead jazz. Other terms used for this broad category of styles include "avant-garde," "creative improvised music," "new music" and "new thing" (a now outdated 1960s phrase used to describe music on the cutting edge). There's no way that we can do justice to the vast world of free jazz here, but it's still worth a quick overview. If you wish to incorporate free jazz into your own music, the information in this section should provide you with a jumping-off point.

The late 1950s saw the development of what we now call free jazz. Some artists, such as Lennie Tristano and Charles Mingus, incorporated elements of free improvisation or unusual dissonance into music that was otherwise somewhat traditional in nature. Others, like Cecil Taylor and Ornette Coleman, were fully committed to exploring the possibilities of free music. Reactions were mixed: to some, Taylor and Coleman were visionaries, showing the way to musical enlightenment; while to others, what they did didn't even qualify as music, much less jazz. While opinions of the genre are still split, these artists are now universally recognized as important figures in jazz, and no one can deny their artistry and vast influence. Furthermore, some of their innovations have carried over into more straight-ahead styles.

If free jazz was born in the 1950s, it came of age in the 1960s, with the emergence of such giants as Anthony Braxton, Albert Ayler, Archie Shepp, Muhal Richard Abrams and Sun Ra. Some of these artists, like keyboardist/bandleaders Abrams and Sun Ra, gravitated to free music from more straight-ahead forms. Meanwhile, some players incorporated free elements into a modern straight-ahead setting, a group that includes Coleman sidemen Charlie Haden, Billy Higgins, Ed Blackwell and Dewey Redman. John Coltrane's music became freer and freer until his death in 1967. Miles Davis's 1960s ensemble with Wayne Shorter, Herbie Hancock, Ron Carter and Tony Williams explored avant-garde elements on both original tunes and standards. Other musicians who added free elements to their sound include pianists Jaki Byard and Mal Waldron, woodwind players Rahsaan Roland Kirk, Sam Rivers, Eric Dolphy and Jackie McLean, trombonist Grachan Moncur III, bassist Dave Holland and drummer Joe Chambers.

Let's look at some of the elements to consider when beginning to play free.

Repertoire

- **Standards:** Use free devices on a standard either selectively or for a whole interpretation.

- **Free tunes:** Some tunes, like many of Coleman's, are loosely structured to enable freedom.

- **No tunes:** Just start playing. Tune in and let the spontaneity of the moment be your guide.

Musical Elements

- **Melody and harmony:** As is true in non-diatonic playing, lyricism is crucial in free music. What's different is the harmonic context, which may be a simple, ambiguous vamp or may even be non-existent. The sky is the limit when it comes to note choices.

- **Rhythm and tempo:** These elements can be approached as in any other jazz situation, though you can use them with greater flexibility. A whole tune, for example, can be played *rubato* (with a free, flexible tempo), or the entire band can change tempos or grooves, as Davis's band did at the club, Plugged Nickel (live recordings are available).

- **Interaction:** This is one of free music's most wide-reaching contributions. With the removal of structure, tuned-in interaction among band members becomes even more crucial. This principle can carry over beyond free music, as in Davis's 1960s band or Bill Evans's trios.

- **Energy:** This takes a place alongside melody, harmony and rhythm. In the music of Cecil Taylor, for example, the sheer energy is as significant as any other aspect.

- **Texture and sound:** Each instrument offers its own special sonic possibilities. On a piano, for example, you can play normally, pluck or dampen the strings, use the pedals in a number of ways and exploit the wide range that's available to you.

The changes in example 247 are in the style of a common progression used by Jerome Kern in the standard "All the Things You Are." More modern tunes with the same changes include Kenny Dorham's "Prince Albert," Bill Evans's "Are You All the Things" and Charles Mingus's "All the Things You Could Be by Now if Sigmund Freud's Wife Was Your Mother." The sample solo's note choices come from a "free" perspective, though parts of the final A section (bars 25–36) correspond more clearly with the changes. The results are sometimes lyrical, sometimes angular and dissonant.

CONCEPTUAL CORNER:
TUNES

If jazz were an entirely mathematical endeavor, you could learn to improvise brilliantly without ever learning a single tune. After all, if it were all math, all of the intangibles (expressivity, for example) would be out of the mix, and you'd be left only with chord changes to negotiate as deftly as possible. If you practiced negotiating every combination of chords that was mathematically possible, you'd theoretically be prepared to shred any changes in an actual tune. By this logic, a brilliant solo on "Body and Soul" or "I Can't Get Started" wouldn't require any particular connection with the tune, since thorough practice would have sufficiently prepared you for the changes. While this level of thoroughness is indeed beneficial, jazz is, of course, more than math. Even if you can shred through any set of changes, there is ultimately no way to get around knowing tunes.

Still have doubts? Try this experiment. The next time you're at a birthday party and people are about to sing "Happy Birthday," whip out your keyboard and say, "The heck with the melody—just let me go straight to the solo!" While it's possible that you'll win everyone over with your change-shredding prowess, that outcome is unlikely. The fact is that people relate to songs, and that alone is reason enough to put your improvisation in the context of a good tune.

The good news is that learning tunes isn't just the musical equivalent of the stuff you have to eat before you can have dessert. Many styles of jazz rely greatly on stating, embellishing and otherwise playing around the melody to a song. This isn't simply because those players lack more sophisticated means of improvisation; indeed, really digging into a song is an important means of giving soul to a performance, and both players and listeners have always preferred soulful musicians to musical mathematicians. "Soulful," in this case, refers not to specific conventions of blues-drenched music, but to the ability to make a passionate, personal musical statement, whatever form that may take.

Many jazz legends—including Earl Hines, Lester Young, Art Tatum, Thelonious Monk, Dexter Gordon, Sonny Rollins and Miles Davis—are revered for their ability to master the techniques and theory of improvisation while remaining "true to the song." If these legends took time to learn tunes and learn them well, what excuse do any of us have for not doing the same? Playing identical lines every time a 12-bar blues is called may be functional, but it's nothing that a well-programmed computer can't do. On the other hand, there is great soulful potential in tuning into the nuances that distinguish "After Hours," "C Jam Blues," "Blue Monk" and "Billie's Bounce" from one another. We've already discussed melodic embellishment (see pages 30–31), but you'll be delighted to see the other, more subtle elements you'll invariably tap into when you embrace the task of learning tunes. Lester Young's now-legendary admonition to use solos to "tell a story" is difficult to heed when playing a tune learned half-heartedly.

Having looked at some of the musical reasons for learning tunes, it's also important to note a very practical reason for doing so: Even the most mathematically inclined musicians will concede that for most skills to be fully integrated, they need to be used when playing with others. Unless you're playing in a context of completely improvised music ("free music," as opposed to the various forms of straight-ahead jazz), you'll need to know tunes. Of course, there are fake books and lead sheets from which you can read a tune. While these are great to have as a safety net, they're no substitute for actually knowing the tunes.

It's a lot harder to be fully involved in music and all its interactive nuances when your face is buried in a music stand. Also keep in mind that many musicians use repertoire as a yardstick by which to measure competence and dedication. The foremost measure, of course, is how you sound, but not knowing many tunes (or even the most "standard" standards) can reflect poorly on you. Some musicians might logically conclude that if you took the music seriously, there's no way you possibly couldn't know "All the Things You Are" or "Stella By Starlight." Conclusions like these can be misleading, superficial, irrelevant or downright false, but people make them just the same, and it's important that none of us close the doors on our learning opportunities.

How to Learn Tunes

If you've made it to this page, you probaly understand how important and beneficial it is to learn tunes. Now, we'll move on from the *why* to the *how*. As part of learning a tune, there are certain elements we must identify and understand: melody, changes and form. On some level, if you learn these elements, you've learned the tune. At the same time, there often isn't a single correct way to play a tune. Traditionally, the correct way to play a tune is the way in which the composer intended it to sound. On a practical level, the correct way to play a tune is however your bandleader wants you to play it. A tune can also be thought of as a means of expression, and therefore, it's entirely up to you as to how it should be interpreted. Naturally, these different viewpoints may at times contradict one another; in some cases, the original changes were not designed or intended for improvisation, while fake books reflect the changes used by jazz musicians. Thankfully, it's possible to learn tunes in a way that addresses all of these issues.

The key to learning a tune is thoroughness. Circumstances will sometimes require that you learn a tune quickly, and in such cases you can only trust whatever sources you have access to. Cross-referencing, however, will deepen your knowledge of a tune, and it is perhaps the key factor in being able to play a tune in any situation. You can learn a tune by ear from a recording, by using a lead sheet or sheet music or by having another musician teach it to you. It stands to reason that if you combine these tactics, you'll be doing a more thorough job. In the case of a standard like "Embraceable You," for example, you'll find numerous recorded versions, a variety of lead sheets and a slew of musicians who can teach you the tune the way they learned it.

There are two points to keep in mind during the process of cross-referencing, each of which will deepen your knowledge of a tune. First, cross-referencing is a means of reinforcement. With each new lead sheet or recording, you internalize the song more fully; you may even find that you learn the lyrics without even trying. Second, you'll often find that cross-referencing unearths a conflict of opinion. You may find a section of a tune in which three different sets of changes are used, or where the melody is not consistently the same. There are number of ways to deal with this issue. First, look for the common ground between the conflicting versions, and try to determine the most basic or straight version. Differing changes often arise from the use of substitutions, so look for the basic changes that provide the starting point for the substitutions in other versions, and watch for common elements in a melody that are embellished on different recordings. You should always try to know the most basic version of a tune, but you'll also benefit from being familiar with other sources. This can be useful in playing with both hip and not-so-hip musicians. Upon learning "Autumn Leaves," for example, you may learn that most jazz musicians play it in the key of G Minor, even though one fake book shows it as being in E Minor. If you see your bandleader opening up that fake book, you can adjust quickly without having to embarrass the boss. On the same tune many people use a particular vamp as an introduction. If you're cross-referenced thoroughly, you'll know what to do if your band mates play this vamp.

For the most thorough reinforcement of a tune, it's helpful to analyze it and play it in all 12 keys. It's difficult to learn every version of every tune, so the next best thing is to be in a position to easily adapt. If you encounter a new set of substitutions on "I Should Care," you'll be prepared if you know the tune well, know where and when it modulates, and so on. Likewise, you never know what key a tune might be called in, especially when working with vocalists. If you're in the habit of 12-keying all the tunes you learn, playing a tune in a new key shouldn't present any problem.

Then, there's the question of which tunes you should learn through the processes described above. The answer is to learn the tunes you need to know in order to survive and thrive. This will vary depending on the situation and environment, but in any case, you'll want to compile a list of tunes to learn. For some, this list will consist almost entirely of standards, while in some crowds, anyone with a repertoire of fewer than ten Wayne Shorter tunes will be dismissed as tragically unhip. The list on page 137 includes some of the most standard tunes in several categories.

Types of Tunes

Several broad categories of tunes provide the basis of any jazz musician's essential repertoire. As with any attempt to dissect and define jazz, these categories are somewhat arbitrary, and some tunes won't fit neatly into any single category. Still, thinking about these categories will help you assemble a useful, diverse repertoire.

Standards

While the literal meaning of "standard" is any tune that's part of the standard repertoire, the tunes most commonly considered standards are those written by such Tin Pan Alley composers as Richard Rodgers, Irving Berlin, Jerome Kern, Cole Porter, Harold Arlen and George Gershwin, or by such honorary members of this club as Duke Ellington. Many other tunes have since become part of the standard repertoire, so "standard" has come to generally refer to any tune from the Tin Pan Alley tradition. Standards make up the bulk of the jazz repertoire and provide the changes and song forms that are often the basis for improvisation, as well as for many other, more modern tunes.

Many standards can be played at a variety of tempos, though some are most often associated with a particular tempo. "Lover" and "Cherokee," for example, are typically played at very bright tempos, while "My Funny Valentine" and "Darn That Dream" are typically played as slow ballads. Knowing a variety of tunes from different tempo/feel categories is always helpful. You should come to know, for example, some tunes that are generally played as ballads, some that are generally played fast, some that are generally played with a Latin feel, and so on.

Blues

A decent repertoire of blues tunes (especially 12-bar blues tunes) is indispensable for a jazz musician. The blues are at the core of nearly all jazz, and blues tunes can be found in all periods and sub-styles within jazz. Not surprisingly, you'll find much overlap among categories—modern blues, bebop blues, and so on.

Bebop

When it comes to tunes, "bebop" generally refers to those that have loping, syncopated melody lines that fit over standard-type chord progressions, usually played at fast tempos. This is especially clear-cut in the fast numbers of bebop giants like Charlie Parker and Bud Powell, while in some cases the bebop designation may seem less apt. Dizzy Gillespie, for example, was undoubtedly a bebop innovator, and many of his tunes, including "Shaw 'Nuff," "Groovin' High" and "Bebop," comfortably wear the bebop label; at the same time, songs like "Con Alma" and "Olinga" have little to do with bebop. On the other hand, composers like Clifford Brown and Horace Silver are associated with bebop much less often than Gillespie is, even though some of their tunes have a distinct bebop feel. While some readily think of tunes like Brown's "Daahoud" and "Joy Spring" and Silver's "Quicksilver" and "Room 608" as genuine bebop, others do not. The key is to be aware of such ambiguities, so that if you're in a position where a "bebop tune" is needed, you're prepared with the knowledge that such definitions may differ.

Modern "Standards"

This is largely a catchall category, a place for tunes that are otherwise hard to pin down. For those who think of standards mainly as old-school tunes by show-tune composers, a different category is necessary for standard-like, often-played tunes by more modern composers like Thelonious Monk and Sonny Rollins. Some of these tunes may resemble bebop, and many, if not all, rely on the ii–V–Is and similar harmonic devices found in Tin Pan Alley tunes.

Modern: Modal and Non-Diatonic

This final category covers modern tunes by modern composers. While the category above covers tunes that behave like standards, these kinds of tunes are written and played from a distinctly modern conception. There is plenty of room for a gray area occupied by the many tunes that are more modern than a standard but still not entirely non-diatonic.

Recommended Tunes by Category

Standards

Alone Together
All of Me
All the Things You Are
Autumn Leaves
Body and Soul
But Not for Me
Bye Bye Blackbird
Caravan
Cherokee
Embraceable You
God Bless the Child
Green Dolphin Street
Have You Met Miss Jones
How High the Moon
I'll Remember April
I Love You
Invitation
I Remember You
I Should Care
Just Friends
Love For Sale
Lover
Misty
My Funny Valentine
Night and Day
Old Devil Moon
Out of Nowhere
Satin Doll
Softly as in a Morning Sunrise
Someday My Prince Will Come
Stella by Starlight
Summertime
Take the "A" Train
There Is No Greater Love
There Will Never Be Another You
What Is This Thing Called Love?
What's New?
You Don't Know What Love Is
You Stepped Out of a Dream

Blues Melodies

All Blues
Au Privave
Bags' Groove
Billie's Bounce
Blue Monk
Blues for Alice
Footprints
Mr. P. C.
Stolen Moments
Straight, No Chaser
Tenor Madness

Bebop

A Night in Tunisia
Bebop
Confirmation
Dig
Donna Lee
Groovin' High
Little Willie Leaps
Scrapple from the Apple
Woody 'n' You

Modern "Standards"

Afro Blue
Blue Bossa
Blue in Green
Ceora
Con Alma
Epistrophy
Four
Giant Steps
Girl from Ipanema
Hi-Fly
In Your Own Sweet Way
Joy Spring
Lady Bird
Lullaby of Birdland
Minority
Moanin'
Oleo
'Round Midnight
St. Thomas
Seven Steps to Heaven
Tune Up
Up Jumped Spring
Voyage
Well, You Needn't

Modern (modal and non-diatonic)

Deluge
Dolphin Dance
E.S.P.
Forest Flower
Freedom Jazz Dance
Inner Urge
Little Sunflower
Maiden Voyage
Miles (aka Milestones)
Nardis
Nefertiti
One-Finger Snap
Passion Dance
So What/Impressions (same harmony)
Witch Hunt

CONCEPTUAL CORNER:
ON-THE-JOB TRAINING
Playing Out, Playing with a Group and the Art of Hanging Out

Learning jazz is like learning to ride a bicycle or to walk: You gather information, try it out, fall down, take your lumps, learn something and try again. While there's much to be said for being prepared for any playing situation, it isn't practical to quarantine yourself in a practice room until you've achieved musical perfection. This is because many of the most crucial lessons in jazz can only be learned by playing with other people. Doing so regularly will keep you on the right path, ensuring that you're practicing and reinforcing the necessary skills.

As soon as you're able to make it through a decent handful of tunes, you should make every effort to play with others. Try to find other players who are at or near your development level. Ask around, put an ad in the paper, put up signs at a music store or school—be industrious. Try also to do some playing with musicians who are better and more experienced than you are. Many towns have jazz jam sessions, which can be great for meeting and playing with other musicians of varying skill levels. If you've already done these things and feel that you need to move on, it's time to actively seek out the players with whom you want to play.

Then there are gigs. Meeting and interacting with musicians—establishing musical contacts—means that some of these musicians may call you to perform with them. If they like your playing, they may even pass your name on to others. At the same time, if you're able to get gigs of your own, you may have the opportunity to hire musicians with whom you want to play. (For more on the practical side of gigging, check out *The Pro Keyboardist's Handbook* by Jon Dryden, published by Workshop Arts/Alfred Publishing.) The main point is that performing in front of an audience can be both gratifying and educational. As important as practicing is, the things you learn on the bandstand will likely resonate more deeply than the things you learn in a practice room.

Though playing in challenging situations is an essential and irreplaceable part of the learning process, knowing how much of a challenge to take on can be tricky. Bear in mind that there are extreme cases. Let's say, for example, you've only learned to play 7th chords in the past month and you get a call to play with a great saxophonist who has been playing professionally for 30 years. By accepting this gig, you'd likely be getting in over your head, something that might damage to your reputation. While it's important to keep possibilities like this in mind, there are relatively few situations in which such choices are necessary. Just be prepared in case they *are*.

While your musical skills are paramount, good personal skills are also vital. How would you feel about a musician who showed up late, dressed like a slob, insulted the club owner and spent the gig watching a football game on television while playing? You wouldn't hire that person, and most likely you'd warn your friends to steer clear of such a person. At a minimum, it's essential that you be punctual, pleasant and appropriately dressed (if you're unsure what's appropriate in a certain situation, ask), and then do your job as well as you can. A big part of success in jazz is simply showing up and not acting like a jerk. You may be a great player, but if people find you difficult to deal with, you'll likely spend a lot of time at home next to a silent telephone. On the other hand, if you're still working on some skills and lack experience but are a cool person with a good attitude, many people will cut you some slack and even help you out. The choice is pretty clear.

Finally, simply hanging out with other jazz musicians is an essential part of your development. (Don't worry; you can still keep your non-jazz-musician friends.) For one thing, opportunities like gigs and informal jam sessions are more plentiful for someone who is "on the scene." If people don't see you around, they're less likely to think of you. More importantly, there's much to be learned from hanging out with other musicians. Interacting with fellow musicians can be enriching in unique ways, and this mode of learning is as old as jazz itself. Also, because jazz is such a social form of music, hanging out off the bandstand often enriches the musical relationships that are so important on the bandstand. You'll inevitably meet some musicians who you don't like much as people, but you'll also meet some soulful, creative people who just might change your life.

CONCLUSION

Here we are, dozens of lessons later, at the end of *The Big Book of Jazz Piano Improvisation*. The end of this book is just the beginning of your improvisational journey. If you've mastered everything we've covered, you certainly deserve some praise. Still, you've hardly reached the end. The reality is that in jazz, there is no end, and while this fact can be humbling, the infinite nature of jazz study is also what makes it so stimulating. The possibilities are truly endless, and there's always another level to reach, which means you'll never need to stop learning or settle for boredom. Duke Ellington, Mary Lou Williams, Dizzy Gillespie, Charles Mingus, John Coltrane, Miles Davis, Dexter Gordon, Art Pepper—the list of jazz musicians who reached great musical pinnacles and could have rested on their laurels, yet continued to grow and evolve, goes on and on. If folks of that caliber keep pushing and growing, there's hardly a reason for the rest of us to be complacent with our own music.

We've said it before, but let's reinforce it one more time: The trick now is to keep the skills you've learned in your back pocket, and see how you can use them as you continue to develop your own style. That is what makes jazz improvisation so profound. The techniques and knowledge you have at your disposal are only tools to help you express exactly how you feel in the moment. Many say that the very essence of jazz lies in the uniqueness of a soloist's spontaneous expression. The most encyclopedic knowledge of history, theory and technique doesn't change the fact that you're a unique being with something unique to say. Give 100 people a dictionary, and they'll all speak differently; give 100 people this book, and they'll all play differently. If that weren't so, a 12-bar blues by Earl Hines would sound identical to one by Bud Powell or by Cecil Taylor—after all, they're all using the same 12 pitches. If you develop your skills at the same time you develop your individual voice, that's a significant accomplishment, and you deserve a pat on the back and hearty congratulations. Now, get back to that practice room.

So, goodbye, au revoir, adios, and peace out, y'all…for now. I'm looking forward to seeing and hearing you on the bandstand sometime soon. Here's a little something to dig on the way out.

The "Peace Out, Y'All" Blues

SUGGESTED LISTENING

This book has repeatedly reinforced the need to listen to great jazz. The albums listed here, which represent a wide range of influential styles and artists, will help reinforce the sounds and ideas we've looked at. Since much of the language of jazz comes from non-keyboard instruments, you're encouraged to also pay attention to the other jazz giants that appear on these albums, either as leaders or sidemen; some of these recordings even place little or no emphasis on keyboard solos. Rest assured that this list is only partial, and that there are plenty of other good albums out there. Ask around, keep your eyes peeled, check your local library and do research to find other albums worth listening to. Enjoy your lifetime of aural discovery!

Abrams, Muhal Richard: *1-OQA+19*

Adderley, Cannonball: *Mercy, Mercy, Mercy* (Joe Zawinul, piano)

Alexander, Monty: *Jamboree/Ivory & Steel*

Allen, Geri: *Some Aspects of Water*

Allison, Mose: *Best of Mose Allison*

Armstrong, Louis: *Hot Fives, Vol. 1* (Lil Armstrong, piano)

Baker, Chet: *Quartet Featuring Russ Freeman* (Russ Freeman, piano)

Barron, Kenny: *Live at Bradley's*

Basie, Count: *Complete Decca Recordings 1937–1939*

Bechet, Sidney: *Best of Sidney Bechet* (various pianists)

Beiderbecke, Bix: *Vol. 1: Singin' the Blues* (various pianists)

Beirach, Richie: *Snow Leopard*

Blakey, Art: *Moanin'* (Bobby Timmons, piano)

Bley, Paul: *Open to Love*

Brubeck, Dave: *We're All Together Again (For the First Time)*

Bryant, Ray: *Alone at Montreux*

Buckner, Milt: *Block Chords Parade*

Byard, Jaki: *Solo/Strings*

Carter, Benny: *Further Definitions* (Dick Katz, piano)

Carter, Betty: *The Audience with Betty Carter* (John Hicks, piano)

Charles, Ray: *The Great Ray Charles*

Clark, Sonny: *Sonny Clark Trio*

Cole, Nat "King:" *Hit That Jive, Jack*

Coleman, Ornette: *Change of the Century* (no piano)

Coltrane, Alice: *Ptah the El Daoud*

Coltrane, John: *A Love Supreme* (McCoy Tyner, piano)

Coltrane, John: *Blue Train* (Kenny Drew, piano)

Contemporary Piano Ensemble: *Four Pianos for Phineas* (Geoff Keezer, Harold Mabern, Mulgrew Miller and James Williams, piano)

Corea, Chick: *Light as a Feather*

Corea, Chick: *Now He Sings, Now He Sobs*

Crispell, Marilyn: *Amaryllis*

Davis, Miles: *Miles Smiles* (Herbie Hancock, piano)

Davis, Miles: *Relaxin' with the Miles Davis Quintet* (Red Garland, piano)

Davis, Miles: *Someday My Prince Will Come* (Wynton Kelly, piano)

DeFrancesco, Joey: *Philadelphia Connection: A Tribute to Don Patterson*

Dolphy, Eric: *At the Five Spot No. 1* (Mal Waldron, piano)

Donaldson, Lou: *Alligator Boogaloo* (Lonnie Smith, organ)

Douglas, Dave: *Soul On Soul* (Uri Caine, piano)

Earland, Charles: *Living Black*

Evans, Bill and Jim Hall: *Undercurrent*

Evans, Bill: *Sunday at the Village Vanguard*

Fitzgerald, Ella with Duke Ellington: *Ella at Duke's Place*

Flanagan, Tommy and Hank Jones: *Our Delights*

Garner, Erroll: *Concert by the Sea*

Getz, Stan and Oscar Peterson: *Stan Getz and the Oscar Peterson Trio*

Goodman, Benny: *After You've Gone* (Teddy Wilson, piano)

Goodman, Benny: *Sextet 1939–1941, Featuring Charlie Christian* (various pianists)

Gordon, Dexter: *Bouncin' with Dex* (Tete Montoliu, piano)

Hancock, Herbie: *Maiden Voyage*

Harrell, Tom: *Form* (Danilo Perez, piano)

Harris, Eddie: *The In Sound* (Cedar Walton, piano)

Hawes, Hampton: *Blues for Bud*

Hines, Earl: *Piano Man*

Hines, Earl: *Live at the New School*

Holiday, Billie: *Complete Decca Recordings* (various pianists)

Holmes, Richard "Groove:" *Blue Groove*

Hope, Elmo: *Homecoming!*

Hubbard, Freddie: *Sweet Return* (Joanne Brackeen, piano)

Hutcherson, Bobby: *Dialogue* (Andrew Hill, piano)

Ibrahim, Abdullah (aka Dollar Brand): *Ancient Africa*

Jamal, Ahmad: *At the Pershing: But Not For Me*

Jamal, Ahmad: *Awakening*

Jarrett, Keith: *Tokyo '96*

Jarrett, Keith: *The Köln Concert*
  Jazzmobile All Stars (Billy Taylor, piano)

Johnson, J.J.: *Let's Hang Out*
  (Stanley Cowell and Renee Rosnes, piano)

Kirk, Roland: *I Talk to the Spirits*
  (Horace Parlan, piano)

Kuhn, Steve: *Countdown*

Lateef, Yusef: *Live at Pep's* (Mike Nock, piano)

Lewis, Ramsey: *The In Crowd*

Louiss, Eddy and Michel Petrucciani: *Conference de Presse*

Mance, Junior: *Happy Time*

Marsalis, Branford: *Requiem* (Kenny Kirkland, piano)

McDuff, Jack: *Live*

McGriff, Jimmy: *I've Got a Woman*

McKenna, Dave: *Dancing in the Dark*

McLean, Jackie: *Let Freedom Ring*
  (Walter Davis, Jr., piano)

McPartland, Marian: *Live at Shanghai Jazz*

McRae, Carmen: *Great American Songbook*
  (Jimmy Rowles, piano)

Mingus, Charles: *Mingus Dynasty*
  (Sir Roland Hanna, piano)

Mingus, Charles: *Changes One* (Don Pullen, piano)

Mobley, Hank: *Messages*
  (Barry Harris and Walter Bishop, Jr., piano)

Modern Jazz Quartet: *Django* (John Lewis, piano)

Monk, Thelonious: *Thelonious Monk Trio*

Monk, Thelonious: *Monk Alone: The Complete Columbia Solo Studio Recordings, 1962–1968*

Montgomery, Wes: *Incredible Jazz Guitar*
  (Tommy Flanagan, piano)

Morton, Jelly Roll: *The Library of Congress Recordings, Vol. 1*

Newborn, Phineas: *The Great Jazz Piano of Phineas Newborn, Jr.*

Navarro, Fats: *Fats Navarro with Tadd Dameron (Live)*
  (Tadd Dameron, piano)

Nichols, Herbie: *Complete Blue Note Recordings*

Parker, Charlie: *Complete Savoy Masters* (various pianists)

Parker, Charlie and Dizzy Gillespie: *Bird and Diz*
  (Thelonious Monk, piano)

Pearson, Duke: *Wahoo*

Pepper, Art: *Tokyo Encore* (George Cables, piano)

Peterson, Oscar: *Trio Plus 1*

Powell, Bud: *Best of Bud Powell* (Blue Note)

Powell, Bud: *Genius of Bud Powell*

Puente, Tito: *Live at the Village Gate* (Hilton Ruiz, piano)

Reinhardt, Django: *Verve Jazz Masters 38* (various pianists)

Rollins, Sonny: *Night at the Village Vanguard* (no keyboard)

Rollins, Sonny: *Sonny Rollins Plus 4* (Richie Powell, piano)

Russell, George: *Ezz-Thetics*

Scott, Shirley: *Queen of the Organ*

Shearing, George: *George Meets the Lion*

Shorter, Wayne: *Juju* (McCoy Tyner, piano)

Shorter, Wayne: *Speak No Evil* (Herbie Hancock, piano)

Silver, Horace: *Blowin' the Blues Away*

Silver, Horace: *Horace Silver Trio*

Smith, Bessie: *Essential Bessie Smith*
  (James P. Johnson and others, piano)

Smith, Jimmy: *Back at the Chicken Shack*

Smith, Jimmy: *Organ Grinder Swing*

Smith, Willie "the Lion": *Memoirs*

Solal, Martial and Johnny Griffin: *In & Out*

Stitt, Sonny and Don Patterson:
  Brothers 4

Sun Ra: *Greatest Hits*

Tatum, Art (with Roy Eldridge, etc.):
  Tatum Group Masterpices Vol. 2

Tatum, Art: *Piano Starts Here*

Taylor, Cecil: *Silent Tongues*

Taylor, Cecil: *World of Cecil Taylor*

Three Sounds: *Babe's Blues* (Gene Harris, piano)

Tjader, Cal and Eddie Palmieri: *Sonido Nuevo*

Tristano, Lennie and Warne Marsh: *Intuition*

Tristano, Lennie: *New Tristano*

Tyner, McCoy: *The Real McCoy*

Valdes, Chucho: *Live at the Village Vanguard*

Vaughan, Sarah: *Sarah Vaughan with Clifford Brown*
  (Jimmy Jones, piano)

Waller, Fats: *Handful of Keys*

Weston, Randy: *Khepera*

Williams, Jessica: *Higher Standards*

Williams, Mary Lou: *Live at the Cookery*

Tony Williams Lifetime : *Spectrum: The Anthology*
  (Larry Young, organ)

Woods, Phil: *Into the Woods*
  (Bill Charlap, Jim McNeely and Hal Galper, piano)

Young, Larry: *Unity*

CD SUPPLEMENT 12-KEY EXAMPLES

In addition to the tracks based on the music in the book, the CD that comes with this book also includes some tracks to help you practice your improvisation in all 12 keys. There is no keyboard on these tracks. The comping is provided by the guitar which is isolated to one channel so that you can tune it out (use your CD player's balance control) and have the experience of playing in a trio with bass and drums. If you don't want to worry about playing the chords all by yourself or if you're a non-keyboardist secretly using this book for soloing, you can leave the guitar in. Be creative and diverse in choosing what to practice on these tracks. For a 12-key review, look at page 22. Note: Each of these progressions begins in the key of B♭.

II–V–I PROGRESSIONS

81

Example 248A: Two-measure, medium tempo ii–V–I progression, moving through the descending cycle of 5ths.

82

Example 248B: Two-measure, medium-up-tempo ii–V–I progression, moving up by a half step on each chorus.

83

Example 249A: Three-measure, medium-tempo ii–V–I progression, moving up by a half step on each chorus.

Example 249B: Three-measure, medium-up-tempo ii–V–I progression, moving through the descending cycle of 5ths.

LONGER PROGRESSIONS

Examples 250–253 will provide you with some tune-length opportunities to play through all the keys. Note that in each of these examples, the turnarounds at the ends of the progressions are altered on each chorus to lead to the new key. For example, if the last measure of a B♭ blues would normally contain an F7 chord, it would in this case contain the V chord of the next key in the progression. So, if moving by descending 5ths, the last measure of this progression would use B♭7 (the V7 of the next key, E♭); if moving up by half steps, the last measure would use F♯7 (the V7 of the next key, B).

250
85

Medium-tempo blues (12 bars), moving up a half step on each chorus, using the changes from example 96 on page 49. (Note that example 96 shows two choruses, while here we'll use only one chorus per key).

251
86

Medium up-tempo blues (12 bars), moving through the descending cycle of 5ths, using the changes from example 250 above.

252
87

Medium up-tempo "Rhythm" changes (32 bars), moving up a half step on each chorus. (See changes in example 155 on page 73; use the basic changes given.)

253
88

Up-tempo "Cherokee"-style changes (64 bars), moving through the descending cycle of 5ths. (See changes in example 156 on pages 74–75.

INDICES

INDEX OF COMPLETE CHORD PROGRESSIONS

INDEX OF SELECTED TOPICS

If you enjoyed
t h i s b o o k . . .
you'll love our school.

National Keyboard
W O R K S H O P
1-800-234-6479

C l a s s e s a r e a v a i l a b l e i n
all styles and levels.
D e s i g n a c o u r s e o f s t u d y
that fits your needs.

Study keyboard, recording technology
or composition in an
intensive but friendly environment.
There are over six campuses
to choose from including
Connecticut, Nashville, Orlando,
Austin, California and Toronto.

Students of all ages enjoy
learning from our outstanding faculty
and working in our
state-of-the-art recording facilities
in week-long summer sessions.

Rock

Jazz

Composition

Blues

MIDI

World Percussion

Guitar

Songwriting

Voice

Digital Media

Drums

Bass

Recording
Technology